D1452616

DISCARDED BY
MT. LEBANON PUBLIC LIBRARY

THE SANCTITY OF DISSENT

Mt. Lebanon Public Library
16 Castle Shannon Boulevard
Pittsburgh, PA 15228-2252
412-531-1912
www.mtlebanonlibrary.org.

THE SANCTITY OF DISSENT

PAUL JAMES TOSCANO

Purchased with funds from the
Allegheny Regional Asset District

SIGNATURE BOOKS   SALT LAKE CITY

1 9 9 4

289.332
T67

MT. LEBANON PUBLIC LIBRARY

AUG 0 7 2008

Cover design by Ron Stucki
Cover photo illustration by John Rees

—

∞ *The Sanctity of Dissent* was printed on acid-free paper
and meets the permanence of paper requirements of the
American National Standard for Information Sciences.
This book was composed, printed, and
bound in the United States.

© 1994 by Signature Books, Inc. All rights reserved.
Signature Books is a registered trademark of
Signature Books, Inc.

98   97   96   95   94   6   5   4   3   2   1

Library of Congress Cataloging-in-Publication Data
Toscano, Paul, date
The sanctity of dissent / Paul James Toscano.
p.   cm.
ISBN 1-56085-049-3
1. Church of Jesus Christ of Latter-Day Saints—Controversial literature.
2. Mormon Church—Controversial literature.
3. Ex-church members—Mormon Church—Religious life.
I. Title.
BX8645.T675   1994
289.3'32—dc20   94-26589
                                      CIP

JJ

SDG

And the word of the Lord came unto me, saying,

Son of man, prophesy against the shepherds of Israel, prophesy, and say unto them, Thus saith the Lord God unto the shepherds: Woe be to the shepherds of Israel that do feed themselves! should not the shepherds feed the flocks?

Ye eat the fat, and ye clothe you with the wool, ye kill them that are fed: but ye feed not the flock.

The diseased have ye not strengthened, neither have ye healed that which was sick, neither have ye bound up that which was broken, neither have ye brought again that which was driven away, neither have ye sought that which was lost; but with force and with cruelty have ye ruled them. . . .

For thus saith the Lord God; Behold, I, even I, will both search my sheep, and seek them out. . . .

I will feed my flock, and I will cause them to lie down, saith the Lord God.

I will seek that which was lost, and bring again that which was driven away, and will bind up that which was broken, and will strengthen that which was sick . . .

—EZEKIEL 34:1-4, 11, 15-16

Contents

PROLOGUE

The essays collected in this book—originally written as speeches—are personal milestones in a journey into exile—a journey that formally began on 16 March 1963 when, as a seventeen-year-old convert from Catholicism, I was baptized a member of the Church of Jesus Christ of Latter-day Saints in the California Baldwin Park II Ward. That journey lasted thirty years and six months, culminating on 19 September 1993, with my excommunication by the stake presidency and high council of the Salt Lake City Big Cottonwood Stake.

Growing up I was never a rebel. I was all obedience and responsibility. And in my early years in the church, my views seemed thoroughly orthodox, and my loyalty to leaders seemed unshakable. But, from the beginning, there was something at the root of my religious life that made my ultimate excommunication highly likely, if not inevitable. This something was not—as some have conjectured—anger, nor ambition, nor amorality, nor arrogance. It was a fundamentally different understanding of the meaning of the restoration of the gospel of Jesus Christ. The essays collected here serve as a chronicle of my progressive development and articulation of this perception of Mormonism that so radically differs from that currently advanced by the mainstream and corporate church.

Modern Mormonism asserts that the purpose of the restoration is to eliminate religious uncertainty by establishing a church and priesthood structure that provides a sure-fire, fool-proof, and fail-safe conduit to God. What modern Mormonism claims to offer the world is not principally a body of teachings or ordinances or spiritual experiences, but a body of divinely called and appointed church leaders ("the Brethren") who are authorized by God to deliver to us inspired counsel on how to live happy, productive, and respectable lives in this world and how to perfect ourselves in preparation for the celestial world to come. Modern Mormonism, therefore, promises to eliminate the risk of personal error in religious matters. In the church we hear this promise again and again in the form of such catchphrases as:

> To be learned is good, if we first harken to counsel.
> There is safety in following the Brethren.
> Obedience is the first law of heaven.
> When a prophet speaks, the thinking has been done.

Over the fourteen-year period spanned by these essays I became painfully aware that the modern LDS church has become crushingly legalistic. It emphasizes strict adherence to rules. It sees righteousness and spirituality in terms of church membership. It teaches that one's standing before God depends on one's loyalty and obedience to the men in charge. In practice, it contradicts Jesus' teachings that we should have no masters. Its policies are at odds with New Testament and Book of Mormon teachings that our relationship with God is not determined by status—be it race, gender, family, tribe, nation, wealth, office, or circumstance. It stresses incessantly the importance of church and priesthood authority over personal spiritual gifts and experiences. Its members tend to testify of the truth of the church rather than of the gospel, to emphasize the family over the individual soul.

I have never agreed with this form of Mormonism. For me, the restoration was meant to re-establish the truth that our relationship to God is individual, personal, direct, and passionate. Our apostles, prophets, and leaders were meant not to give us rules of conduct, but to call us to Christ. The Brethren were not chosen primarily to receive revelation for us, but to teach us how to obtain revelation for ourselves. For it is not our leaders, but the spirit alone that can confirm in us all truth. The church was not created to save us. The church is what needs to be saved. Its purpose is not to dispense rewards and punishments, but ordinances and teachings by which we may be spiritually transformed. The church was never intended to serve as a shuttle to heaven, but to encourage us on our own spiritual journeys, to teach us that mistakes are inevitable, but that forgiveness is at hand, that God's love for us is personal and unconditional, and that each of us is equally sacred.

This is not to deny or disparage the need for church, family, government, or other social structures. Scripture teaches that each Christian is a living stone in the spiritual temple of God. Structures are important. But they are not primary. They are necessary. But they are not sufficient. The basic building block of any community, religious or otherwise, must be the individual soul, whose worth, the scripture declares, is "great in the sight of God." The ninety and nine must be left for the sake of the one because the individual is always more important than the organization. The congregation is never holier than the humblest of its members. The good news is not that Christ loves the church, but that Christ loves each individual. He died not to spiritually empower the collective, but each child, each woman, each man. Had there been but one sinner, Christ would have died for that one alone. Chief among the radical teachings of Jesus Christ is that God is not a tribal deity at all. God is the God of each person, no matter what her tribe, his nation, her family, his class—no matter what his or her religious understanding.

The modern church is uncomfortable with this view because, down deep, it does not fully trust its members to respond to the spirit of God or to apply the principles of the gospel. It does not fully trust God to do his/her own work. The ecclesiastical bureaucracy doubts the power of God to spiritually transform the rank and file members of the world-wide church. It sees itself as a spiritual elite whose primary duty is to reinforce true worship. So, it makes additions to the gospel message. It makes up rules. It promises those who obey them that they will become citadels of rectitude safe from the vicissitudes of life. For this reason, in the modern church to avoid sin is a more certain course than to repent, to judge rightly more serviceable than to forgive, and to follow the Brethren more reliable than to follow the spirit.

The good news has always terrified the legalistic and controlling, those who demand closure. To them the gospel seems too unpredictable, too risky, too open-ended. Such people find it difficult to trust an invisible God, to shoulder a cross of personal sacrifice, and to assume and allow others to assume the risks of personal accountability to God. Jesus says to us: "Take up your cross and follow me." But we do not want this. We want to lay it down and follow someone else. We want leaders who will make us lists of dos and don'ts, tell us how to dress, when to laugh or cry, what to speak, where to go, whom to trust, what to believe, and why. We want someone to outline our life's plan, a plan of happiness, where everything is pre-scheduled. We want a celestial itinerary worked out by God-appointed travel guides who can give us a map that charts for us a spiritual journey without mistakes, losses, weaknesses, sins, or unpleasantness. In short, we want all the benefits of life and none of its burdens. We want to go back to Eden, away from the lone and dreary world. We want a clean, well-lighted place, perfect, changeless, safe. We want freedom from freedom.

But this is the one freedom God will not allow us. Salvation frees us from bondage not from liberty. Each person is responsible for his or her own spiritual journey, for his or her own failings. No competent person can escape this responsibility. Each individual must choose to make her or his own mistakes or to make the mistakes of someone else. If we make our own, we can grow through repentance. If we do not, we will stagnate in blindness or self-righteousness. No one can dodge this responsibility by transferring it to a spiritual leader. To attempt this is idolatry.

In the course of my journey into exile, I came to accept that the modern church's view of the restoration was irreconcilably opposed to my own. With ever-increasing clarity I saw that the church, in its misguided attempt to create for its members a safe place, instead, was creating for them a prison and abetting abuse. I came to believe that God will not bless such an effort, nor acquiesce in the abdication of our personal responsibility for the spiritual welfare of our own souls, nor smile benignly upon us as we sell ourselves into slavery no matter how well-meaning, or inspired, or authorized our masters may be.

I was excommunicated from the church for publicly expressing these criticisms, which have been collected in this book. These essays trace my spiritual journey away from legalism to redemptive Mormonism. They memorialize the development and articulation of my view that the true purpose of the restoration was not to create yet another "one and only true" group, but to re-establish Christ's "true and living church"—not a closed ecclesiastical corporation, but an open and genuine religious community whose members believe, not merely in the sanctity of the collective, but mainly in the sanctity of personal experience, personal salvation, personal revelation, personal freedom, personal empowerment, and personal accountability to a personal God—a community whose members believe in the sanctity of the individual and in the sanctity of dissent.

Easter 1994

Chapter One.

THE PANDEMIC OF NARCISSISM

"The Pandemic of Narcissism" was originally presented on 29 March 1979 to honors students, faculty, and guests attending the annual closing Honors Program Banquet at Brigham Young University.

It is a strange twist of fate that I have been asked to address you. I was never a member of the Honors Program. Nor was my membership ever solicited. Nor was there ever any reason for my membership to have been solicited. In 1963—in the dark ages when the BYU student body population was about 15,000 strong and freshmen were required to wear beanies during orientation week while registration was accomplished manually in a marathon session in the George Albert Smith Fieldhouse—back then, I accidentally signed up for an honors freshman English course. But someone discovered the mistake, and I was asked to drop the class and take something more in keeping with my achievements. Wounded pride moved me to resist this request. I eventually managed to convince the teacher, John S. Harris, to let me stay and prove myself. This I did in a way. I earned a C. I am not sure I have ever entirely recovered from what was my last encounter with the Honors Program until this evening.

1

So you see why I feel a bit strange speaking here tonight. It reminds me of a little known historical fact. In 1904 the Ogden, Utah, School for the Deaf and Blind joined the Utah Basketball League. They played right along with BYU and the University of Utah. I don't know how they did it. But, certainly, the blind students could not have done the playing. As I reckon it, the deaf students must have played while the blind cheered. Obviously, this arrangement had its drawbacks. Undoubtedly, the cheers of the blind were badly timed. But this probably did not matter much since the players would not have been able to hear them anyway. Perhaps this is how it will be for us. You may not be able to see exactly when I've scored a point, but then again it won't matter much since I am more or less deaf to cheers and catcalls.

Let me begin with an old story. Long ago, in the land of Thespis, Greece, there was born to a nymph an uncommonly beautiful child whom she named Narcissus. The beauty of this child never abated as he grew older; instead, it increased. By age sixteen, Narcissus was probably the most beautiful mortal that had ever graced the world. He was loved and sought after by women and men both, but to no avail. For, though he loved admiration, he rejected all lovers and all friends. He was very proud of his beauty and could find room in his heart only for himself.

A lovely nymph named Echo was among the many whom he rejected; as a result, she dwindled to nothing more than a voice, capable only of repeating the words of others.

One day, while hunting, Narcissus chanced upon a lake whose smooth, sheer surface made a marvelous mirror. Tired and thirsty, Narcissus approached the water's edge to drink, and there he saw his own reflection. It was love at first sight. He reached out and attempted to embrace and kiss himself and presently realized that he was looking at his reflected image. This realization, however, did not deter his fancy. He was enchanted and enraptured. He gloried that he was himself but was grief-stricken that he could not possess himself as he might possess another. This fact tormented him. But he clung to this tormented love, choosing it rather than any means of escape because he believed that he, at least, would remain true to himself, whatever happened.

In some versions of this story, Narcissus, like Echo, pines away and vanishes. In others, he becomes so hopelessly addicted to himself that he, distressed that his self-love can never be requited, plunges a dagger into his bosom saying, "Ah, youth, beloved in vain, farewell." His blood is said to have spilled upon the ground and on his death-place there grew up white and red flowers from which a narcotic extract is distilled. The flower is called the Narcissus to this day.

An analysis of the Narcissus myth provides a nearly complete catalogue of the paradoxical spiritual ills that beset our own generation: a pride in self coupled with a terrible sense of inferiority; an obsession with youth and beauty; an avoidance of genuine love in favor of sentimentality; the proliferation of human relationships that are self-serving, manipulative, and often cruel; an intense demand for fulfillment and admiration coupled with a disregard for admirers; a rejection of whatever does not serve or preserve the self; addictive behaviors and a literal reliance upon narcotics; and a fundamentally suicidal disregard for both the past and the future.

These symptoms of narcissism are so widespread in our day that it may be fairly concluded that narcissism itself has reached pandemic proportions, infecting nearly every facet of life. Few, indeed, are those individuals and institutions that have demonstrated any immunity to it whatsoever. We Mor-

mons, if anything, have demonstrated an unusual suscepti-
bility to it.

Let me say, first, that narcissism should not be confused
with rugged individualism or selfishness. The hallmark of
individualism is independence from the group. Like Henry
David Thoreau, the individualist cares neither for the animosity nor the admiration of the multitude. He or she wants
to be alone, to eat beans in the woods. Narcissism is characterized by dependence on others for admiration and rein-
forcement, which is often unreciprocated or held in contempt. Narcissism freely receives, but cannot freely give. It
does not deal in emotional donations, but in investments
with calculated returns. Thus, narcissism is not mere selfishness; it is its most virulent strain. Selfishness can be mild and
limited, but narcissism is not. The narcissist is not just egotistical or slightly grasping in one or two categories, he is
consumed by an obsession to make all things serve his ends
and fill his needs. It is the narcissist who must survive. He is
not merely trapped in the prison of his ego, it is his obsession
to draw all others into the penitentiary of his own contracted
heart.

A look at today's fads will provide as good an introduc-
tion to the modern effects of narcissism as anything. It was
Christopher Lasch who pointed out that since people no
longer believe that the world can be improved in any significant ways they have resorted to faddish little improvements
calculated to preserve themselves. As Lasch observed in *The
Culture of Narcissism* (New York: Norton & Co., 1978):

> After the political turmoil of the sixties, Americans
> have retreated to purely personal pre-occupations. . . .
> getting in touch with their feelings, eating health food,
> taking lessons in ballet or belly-dancing, immersing

themselves in the wisdom of the East, jogging, learning how to "relate," overcoming the "fear of pleasure" (4).

The narcissistic concern with self-image has made the personal appearance industry the third-largest in the nation. Blow-dry hair, ever-gloss lipstick, deodorants, colognes, the obsession with slim waistlines and expanded chests, all are part and parcel of the cult of self. Also on the popular level is the profusion of sentimental, narcissistic kitsch: the posters and bumper stickers with their assorted aphorisms that are devoid of any intellectual or spiritual content. We are encouraged to cope with the complexity of life by slogans like "This Is the First Day of the Rest of My Life," when it may just as likely be the last day of the first of our life. Or "Every Day in Every Way I Am Getting Better and Better," when the truth is that we are just barely maintaining the status quo. Or "I Am Really Special," when in fact we are quite ordinary. Or "Happiness Is [Fill in the Blank]," as if any human could ever draw sustained happiness from any single source. Or "I Am Unique," as if there were any value in uniqueness without truth or love. Worse yet are the sentimental anecdotes, the stock and trade of both the politicians' platform and the preachers' pulpit, the purpose of which is to pump up emotions while dulling discernment.

An example of such kitsch is the smiley button: the no-face face with its inane admonition to "Have a Nice Day." This is really much more than a casual greeting. It is a form of soft coercion, a demand that everyone smile and be happy. The wearer seeks to be surrounded by smiles without contributing to anyone's genuine happiness. A smile is demanded. But what kind? A mindless grin. The smiley face is a type of modern Gorgon. Picture it: thousands of smiling faces all of stone, and on their foreheads the dark and insulting motto chiseled out in a casual script: "Have a Nice Day."

But I digress. The main concern of popular narcissism is to be admired, to be pleasing. Even popular sports have degenerated from a contest of strength to a contest of strength of personality. Athletes are not as interested in winning as they are in having a winning image, maximum publicity, and a seven figure salary. Of course, Americans want superstars and are willing to pay the price. Only a minority are interested in ideas or current events. The majority is mesmerized by celebrity. That is why *Life* magazine has been replaced by *People* and *Self*. The emphasis today is on people who are admired for no other reason than that they are popular. They are listened to not because they have something important to say, but because they are important and are saying something. Witness the "Tonight Show."

Narcissism has suffused itself into such areas as art, law, politics, education, business, human sexuality, and religion. In the realm of the law, narcissism has led to legal instrumentalism: the idea that the government should create laws not only to prohibit bad acts, but to compel good ones. America is rooted in a tradition of limited government—the idea that government should exist to prevent certain negative behaviors like fraud, murder, theft, conspiracy, not to mandate pre-packaged outcomes. The concept of ordered liberty has degenerated to the concept of ordered order. The narcissistic consciousness of modern America has contributed to the decline of freedom and the rise of the therapeutic state. We have exchanged liberty for security and comfort. This has happened through the politics of narcissism. As citizens, our obsession for self-preservation is translated at the polls into demands for welfare legislation, while our politicians' obsession for admiration and personal power is transformed, in the legislatures, into people-pleasing programs passed to win votes of special interest groups. The vicious cycle begins: the need for celebrity and the demand of self-interest feed on one another. We give lip service to the idea that issues are really at the heart of American politics. But it is clear to nearly everyone now that politics has become a circus of celebrities, gossip, scandals—all centered around the most unworthy of all political concerns, the cult of personality.

Perhaps the direst symptom of the politics of narcissism is the development of a new and ominous concept of authority. Historically, Americans have been imaged as a people ready to resist any encroachment on freedom. But this is not true. Leaders on both left and right are willing to abuse the power of the state in order to achieve certain "moral" outcomes—whether decency or equality. People are willing to ignore power abuses so long as the powerful promise them benefits. Moreover, we tend to tolerate abuses of power and special privilege out of trust for our public and private institutions, even though there is significant evidence that many of these are, in fact, self-serving and untrustworthy. Perhaps we put up with the whip only because we hope to one day hold the whip handle.

Narcissism has also invaded the realm of education. Witness in the public schools the deemphasis on discipline, the focus on fulfillment, the failure to tune-up minds, the obsession with entertainment and technological gimmickry, the concern with image and popularity, the unwillingness to make even reasonable academic demands—in a word, the shallowness.

The effects of narcissism are as bad in the colleges and universities, where a broad liberal education is now deemphasized in favor of "useful" knowledge—which is any information that leads to cash, power, authority, pleasure, and celebrity. A university is no longer a scholarly refuge from the world, but a materialistic microcosm of it. It is not a repository of truth. It is a career advisement center, a recruiting station for the big firms looking either to expand their inventory of human resources or to replace the worn-out parts. The litmus test for a successful university or professional school is the size of the income of its alumni. Money-making abilities are generally considered to be the chief indicia of the educated man. This explains, in part, why university officials are always inviting rich people to address students. It is a practical way of catering to the rich and cultivating them as donors. It is second only to the edifice complex: the practice of erecting for the school grand buildings that bear donors' names, as if the buildings were family mausoleums. Both techniques are accepted ways of manipulating people and of going after the big bucks necessary to keep the institution solvent.

Educational institutions cannot be blamed for this. They are, after all, dealing with the wealthy who so often seek this form of celebrity. As a happy side effect, students are encouraged, by example if not by precept, to seek riches so they, too, will become rich alumni who can be later pursued for further donations. Thus, at the modern university, knowledge is not primarily sought for its own ends, or for the joy of knowing, or for the delight of discovery, but in order to prepare students for careers that will, in due time, redound to the financial benefit of the alma mater. Thus, the emphasis is on first-tier subjects like accounting, business, law, organizational behavior, public administration, and medicine. Second-tier subjects like political science, sociology, statistics, English, foreign languages, science, and technology, are encouraged because they are unavoidable prerequisites to the really "useful" courses. Third-tier subjects like history, classics, ancient studies, philosophy, and theology are considered holdovers from another age (like academic regalia). These are not perceived as contributing in any way to either the university's, the students', or society's positive cash flow. They are endured for the same reason any tradition is endured. They are nostalgic and set institutions of higher learning apart from other corporate entities. Also, it would take more effort to cut out useless courses than it would to let them die a slow death.

Educational utilitarianism gives rise to the faculty degree-seeking game, based on the principle that a Ph.D. is basically a ticket to a job, a higher salary, or greater benefits rather than a sign of competence in research and writing. There is, too, the prevalent practice of many academicians of building their careers on the research and study of their students (a kind of academic pimpery where the student does the dirty work for credit or slave-wages while the professor gets the celebrity and royalties). There are also the soft threats and subtle intimidations exerted on campus small-fry by campus big-fry who are anxious to preserve their own prestige. There is the intellectual dishonesty, pompous posturing, professional double-talk, filibustering, and the ever-present resort to authoritarianism—all of which are used as means to avoid the honest and open exchange of views that is essential to any serious quest for truth, but that is anathema to the narcissistic obsession with self-importance and self-image.

In the realm of business it must be seen that the narcissistic demands for admiration, success, power, and pleasure are demands that can be supplied. Narcissism has become a multi-billion dollar business. The best way to fill one's own need for power, popularity, and money is to supply the needs of others—for a price. Consumerism is viewed as a kind of therapy. If people feel down, they buy something new to bolster their spirits. Advertising has convinced us that products can actually make us cleaner, whiter, smarter, slimmer, sweeter, gladder, grander, tougher, smoother, and more regular—but above all sexier, for in the world of narcissism sexual gratification is the ultimate fulfillment and orgasm is tantamount to the second comforter. If narcissism were a religion, advertising would be its missionary program. The myth lingers on that advertising broadcasts product information to interested consumers. But advertising doesn't spread information; it hides it, slants it, manipulates it. Its purpose is not to inform the market, but to create a market. It does not seek to persuade by argument, but to seduce by sentimentality, emotion, and appeal to our desire for superiority, success, and sex.

It is the narcissistic demand for gratification here and now that makes the national economic picture look dim. People are not willing to sacrifice in the present for a benefit in the future. Conservative investment is out. Pyramid sales and golden circles are in. We are living on tomorrow's wealth. We are consuming tomorrow's resources. We put into our pockets the money that belongs to our posterity. The present is swiftly becoming the future, and that future is already bankrupt. We plan on suicide tomorrow to avoid sacrifice today. It is the ultimate buy now pay later plan. That we are committing economic suicide should not surprise us. Remember the myth of Narcissus.

But the deepest and most pejorative effects of narcissism are on Christianity. These effects can be grouped into the following two categories: (1) the trivialization of redemption and growth of idolatry, and (2) the trivialization of doctrine and emphasis on service and sentimentality.

Christianity is a redemptive religion. It teaches that we

are fallen creatures who must be saved from death and hell by supernatural intervention. The Calvinistic view is that we are not just fallen, but utterly depraved and, thus, incapable even of choosing God or calling for divine help. Jean Calvin taught, therefore, that God had to choose humans. From this idea comes the doctrine of predestination, that God chooses some and not others. Joseph Smith contradicted this view. He taught that although humanity is fallen it is not so depraved that we are incapable of desiring good and choosing God. In fact, in Joseph Smith's view, we are responsible for choosing God as part of our salvation experience. The Mormon position is that, though as humans we are enemies to God, we possess the agency and power to ask for divine help; and we must exercise that agency to receive the grace that reconciles us to God. The first point, then, is that Christianity is a religion that teaches that humans must be redeemed by God's grace or deteriorate into devils.

Modernity denies this fallen condition. It holds that we are either naturally good or capable of solving our own problems. Both views manage to sidestep the sacrifice of a broken heart and contrite spirit—which are, in the Christian view, necessary prerequisites to the divine transformation from spiritual sickness to spiritual health.

Those who believe that we are basically virtuous see God as a lawgiver who, if obeyed, will help maintain our pristine purity. This is religious legalism, a view held by the pharisees and scribes as described in the gospels. For legalists, righteousness is not in Christ, but in the law and the law-abiders. Religion is, therefore, a matter of living the rules—doing good deeds and avoiding bad ones. Repentance is a ritual for regaining one's former purity, rather than a transformation into an altogether new spiritual creature in Christ. Legalism is narcissistic because it denies the need for deep spiritual transformation. The human spirit is seen as essentially good and all that is needed to improve our condition is human reformation based upon re-education and behavioral modification. Legalism denies that we lack the divine power necessary for spiritual perfection.

The other narcissistic alternative to legalism is humanitarianism, which sees salvation in terms of economics, psychiatry, sociology. This view promotes relief, but not joy. It wishes to assuage guilt rather than avoid hell. In this view, immortality is a matter of genetic engineering; eternal life is a matter of psychocybernetics. The shaman, the prophet, the healer are replaced by secular priests—doctors, lawyers, financial managers.

Whether legalistic or humanitarian, the narcissist, though believing, cannot accept a redeemer, cannot relate well to Christ. For him the Messiah is an enigma. A wise man? Yes! A moral teacher? Certainly! The Son of God? Yes—in the sense that we are all sons and daughters of God. But a divine being? No. At best, God is like Zeus, or to paraphrase C. S. Lewis, God is a senile old benevolence who likes to look down and watch his kids having a good time. For the narcissist, God's main role is not that of a divine physician who will cure us from our mortal ills. At best, God is only a cosmic talent scout who roams through the world helping people to develop their inherent potentialities. He is like the genie in Aladdin's lamp, one who can be summoned to grant a wish, fulfill a need, satisfy a fleeting curiosity, or otherwise deliver the goods. At worst, God is a whipping boy upon whom can be blamed the self-made evils of humanity.

In Mormonism we find a curious brand of Christian narcissism. We seem to relate much better to God the Father than to God the Son. We sing again and again the childhood hymn "I am a child of God." We like to remind ourselves of our family connection to the head of the universe. In this way we wish to avoid the harsh teaching that we have been disowned from that family. "If God is my Father," we say, narcissistically, "then I really must be special." Of course, then everyone is special, for everyone is a child of God. But the real message of Christianity and Mormonism is not that God is the Father (pagans believe this, too), but that Christ is Redeemer. The gateway to God is Christ. Though the world is in sin, God so loved the world that he entered the world in the incarnation that through him we might be born again into the divine family. This is the redemptive core of Christianity that is so repugnant to the narcissistic point of view—the need for a redeemer.

Our failure to see Christ as central is the cause of idolatry. Once Christ is out of the shrine something must fill the void: the family, the church, the social programs, the temple, the music, the text, the authority, the ritual, the ethics, the culture. The list goes on. But without Christ, the family becomes the mafia, the church apostatizes, the social programs fail, the temple crumbles, the music becomes banal, the texts become confusing and corrupt, authorities become tyrannical, the ritual becomes meaningless and sentimental, the moral code becomes harsh and inflexible, and the culture putrefies. So long as Christ is the head, the parts of the body of Christ are healthy. When the head is cut off, the parts die. "I am the vine, ye are the branches." We cannot obtain from the bodily parts the enlightenment and life that can only come from the head. It is idolatry to try.

The marginalization of Christ is usually accompanied by the trivialization of doctrine. Narcissism despises Christian doctrine, first, because in order to understand it, one must concentrate on something other than oneself and, second, because Christian doctrine insists on one's fallen nature.

Besides, doctrine is divisive. It brings unpleasantness, which damages image and drives away admirers. There can be no celebrity without admirers.

As we Mormons have become more narcissistic, our attention turns from doctrinal teaching to the telling of anecdotes that encourage obedience and service. What we fail to understand is that the absence of Christian charity is not remedied by the promotion of humanitarian service. The best way to enlist people in the service of others is first to preach the gospel so they can feel their spiritual connection to God. What humanitarians fail to see is that the love of God automatically includes the love of neighbor, but the love of neighbor does not necessarily include the love of God. The greater includes the less, but not vice versa. Narcissism is not interested in the love of God, for that love cannot be subverted to selfish ends. Humanitarian service can. The McDonald's hamburger jingle summed it up: "We do it all for you." But in the background one can hear the ching of the register. Yes, it is easy to serve others to serve ourselves. This is priestcraft: to serve the cause so long as the cause serves us.

Another narcissistic symptom in Mormonism is sentimentality. As G. K. Chesterton observed seventy years ago, when truth quits the field, sentimentality, not error, takes over. Sentimentality was defined by Hugh Nibley as a "tenacious clinging to pleasantries." It is a state of mental torpor characterized by a craving for meaningless but pleasant stories and sayings. It is a craving for emotional experiences without regard to their source, their truth, or their value. The best example I can give of this is a short movie marketed by BYU called "The Sacrifice." The storyline is this: A little boy is hit by a train while walking over a trestle to be with his father, the switchman. The conflict in the story comes when the father must decide whether to let go of the switch and save his little son at the cost of the passenger train or whether to sacrifice his son and save the train. He decides to save the train. At the end of the movie, a caption overlays the closing scene, proclaiming, "And God so loved . . ." Obviously, the film is intended as an atonement analogy. Although well-intentioned (and sentimentality is usually well-intentioned), it succeeds only in being maudlin. It tugs at the heart-strings but does not edify the spirit. Why? Because the analogy is false. Jesus is not a mindless or disobedient child who wandered onto the train trestle of the universe to be accidentally flattened by a blind, indifferent cosmos. God the Father was not a powerless technocrat caught in the press of circumstances beyond his control. The relationship between them was not that of an infant son and a youthful father. The emotions the movie calls forth are nothing like the emotions the real participants felt, as reported by those who knew them best. It is false from top to bottom. Its net effect is to take our attention off truth and fix it upon our own emotions. It seeks only to induce a pleasant sense of spiritual euphoria—the kind of feeling we get when we hear about poor people being helped in far away places, but not like the feeling we get when we actually go to far away places to help the poor. The movie does nothing to further anyone's understanding of the nature of the Father and the Son, or of the Atonement, or of the love of God, or of anything that is spiritually significant.

Whether in the form of films, books, pamphlets, or pulpit rhetoric, sentimentality represents a rejection of truth and love. Its net effect is to bring everybody closer to spiritual brain death—a practically comatose state where the mental powers are dysfunctional, but the heart, as the center of emotion and feeling, goes right on pumping, pumping, pumping. Whether in popular culture, politics, education, or religion, narcissism has powerful effects. How has it become so widespread? Why has it gone unopposed? The reasons are simple, really: It claims to be good for business because it increases sales and profits. It claims to be good for the ego because it assuages guilt without sacrifice. It claims to be good for the powerful because it encourages ambition. In fact, narcissism claims to be good for everybody except the few who want to submit themselves to something higher, better, and other than themselves.

Narcissism is curable. The cure is the coming to us of Christ in the Holy Spirit. To realize the cure, we must accept on some level that salvation lies outside ourselves and is available when we accept the divine powers of heaven that can transform us into new creatures of spiritual maturity.

Dispensing this cure requires us to preach clearly the gospel of Jesus Christ and to distinguish that gospel from the message of narcissism. It is, in my view, important to see and help others to see that:

* Narcissism teaches reliance on self, Christianity teaches reliance on Christ. This is not to denigrate the self, but to say that the self matures only in its recognition of its interdependence with an "other" and with the "Other."

* Narcissism promotes admiration, Christianity promotes love—the unconditional, reciprocal, mutual, specific, and passionate love of an other or others, of God, and of self.

* Narcissism teaches human perfection by humans, Christianity teaches human perfection by God.

* Narcissism seeks human reformation; Christianity, spiritual transformation.

* Narcissism seeks gradual behavioral improvement; Christianity, an invasion of spiritual power into the soul.

* Narcissism seeks to avoid pain, Christianity seeks to endure pain and find meaning in it.

* Narcissism longs for pleasantries, Christianity longs for truth and love, for forgiveness and repentance both in self and in others.

* Narcissism employs nondisclosure, threats, exclusion, and outright force, as well as disinformation, manipulation, flattery, bribes, privilege, and denial while Christianity is based on faith, hope, charity, honesty, equality, spirituality, repentance, and forgiveness.

It is clear that I see narcissism as a spiritual disease of pandemic proportions. I believe that it has infected all aspects of our lives. It has even infected and polluted the holy church of God. In my view, we urgently need to reject the nostrums, placebos, and panaceas so plentiful in the modern world and the modern church, and to accept once and for all the blessed and enduring cure of redemption and spiritual renewal offered to us by the Most High as a free gift.

We are poised at the end of the second millennium. We have no time to trifle with quackery. Though the disease is virulent, the cure is at hand. Let us not reject our salvation now. He has engraved us on the palms of his hands. Let us engrave him on the tablets of our hearts. I commend you to him through the Holy Ghost.

Chapter Two.

BEYOND TYRANNY,
BEYOND ARROGANCE

"Beyond Tyranny, Beyond Arrogance" was originally presented at the Sunstone Theological Symposium in August 1986.

My honeymoon with the Mormon church lasted five years, between 1961 when I converted and 1966 when I left on my proselyting mission. During that period I had had inklings that there was trouble in store for me, but I didn't actually come face to face with it until my final mission interview with my bishop. In order to get my call, I had to lie.

It was a hot California night, and I was at the bishop's house, sitting at the kitchen table, signing the papers that had to be sent to Salt Lake City. Out of the blue he asked me if I had a testimony of Joseph Smith. I assured him that I did, and then I tried to impress him. (I often felt the need to impress church leaders then.) I told him about some research I had done at BYU the previous spring and how I'd learned that Joseph Smith had probably taken his first plural wife as early as 1831.

The bishop went cold. After a full thirty seconds of silence, he said in a voice that was suddenly grave and authoritarian and not quite his own: "Elder, Joseph Smith never practiced polygamy. That is a false teaching of the apostate Reorganized Church."

It took me a few moments to sort out the problem. Several responses ran through my mind. And then I decided to object. But I thought it would be prudent to put my objection in the form of a question: "Bishop," I asked, "isn't it the other way around? Isn't it the Reorganized Church that denies Joseph ever practiced polygamy?"

He never batted an eye. "Elder," he said starkly, "I'm not going to let you serve a mission if you believe in false doctrine and if you have a rebellious attitude."

It was then as I looked into his frowning face that I saw—for the first time—the dark underbelly of ecclesiastical authoritarianism; and I realized that I had a problem. That's when I decided to lie.

"I'm sorry," I said, humbly. "I must have gotten mixed up. I didn't know it was false doctrine. I'm just a convert."

Apparently I hit upon the right tack. The bishop smiled broadly and patted me on the shoulder. "It's best to leave the mysteries alone," he said. "Don't be too sure of yourself, Elder. There is safety in obeying the counsel of your leaders."

I nodded.

"I think there's a lesson for you in this, Elder," he said.

That was true. But it would be a long time before I understood it.

Over the next ten years, my encounters with authoritarianism became more frequent and more unpleasant. But, strangely enough, they never quenched my own lust for power. If anything, they fueled it. I guess, on some obscure and confused level, I had decided that the way to escape church authoritarianism was to become a church authority myself.

My confusion began to clear in the mid-1970s, while I was in law school at BYU studying about order and liberty. During this period I learned about the Lockean school, a group of political philosophers who promulgated the concept of ordered liberty—the idea that political powers are inherent in people and that the sovereign can tap those powers only with popular consent, and only while reserving to individuals the widest possible residuum of rights and powers to achieve their private, social, and economic objectives.

This viewpoint, I learned, was opposed by others for whom ordered liberty seemed inadequate. If people are left free, they asked, will not the strong prey upon the weak? Moral order is essential to happiness. So the counter-concept developed that power is not inherent in individuals but in the community as a whole. This power should be exploited by a chosen (not necessarily democratically chosen) elite with knowledge and experience to carry out the moral objectives of the community. These moral objectives usually take one of two forms: moral decency or equality. If community leaders see some perceived crime, such as pornography, as the most dangerous threat to the community, they use the power of the community to eliminate the criminal element. If inequality is perceived as a threat to the community, then the police power will be used to redistribute wealth or privilege. In either case, moral order is achieved by granting to the sovereign elite the widest possible margin of authority to achieve its social and economic goals and to prevent individuals from creating enclaves of indecency or pockets of privilege.

As I quarried out this information in spoonfuls, I was led to wonder: Is not forced morality the greatest of the immoralities? If a community uses force to promote morality, then how can the community itself be moral? And how can equality be enforced without conferring an unequal amount of power upon the enforcers? Therefore, must not every egalitarian society be, *per force*, an elitist society? My head was buzzing with thoughts of morality, equality, and liberty, and in the end I concluded that the greatest of these is liberty.

These insights altered my love-hate relationship with church authority which, by 1977-78, I had come to despise in the incompetent, but which I still admired in the competent, particularly me—for I was a third-year law student and considered myself one of the most competent persons I knew. Then, quite suddenly, in my last months of law school, I changed my mind. I underwent a paradigm shift. I came to see that authority and power could corrupt even the competent—yes, even me. My watchwords became "Rebellion to tyrants is obedience to God" and "Trust not in the arm of flesh." It was very exhilarating to say these things. And thus it was that in the spring of 1978 I was born again: I became a child of the 1960s. I was late, I know. I'm used to being late. So it didn't embarrass me to join the revolution just after it was over, when everyone else was cashing in its ideals for money market certificates and convertible debentures.

After law school I married Margaret, and my authority problems got worse. This had nothing to do with her. It was just that we didn't seem to fit in anywhere. We both quite *liked* the gospel and liked talking about it. This fact, coupled with some strange rumors about us, led some of our ecclesiastical leaders to conclude that we were simultaneously anti-Mormons, polygamists, and born-again Jesus-freaks. Rather a tall order, even for us. After eight years we can look back at these events and laugh, but at the time these accusations were painful and alienating. During this period, we both realized that we didn't fit into the Mormon mainstream, but our beliefs and loyalties made us reluctant then to see ourselves as Mormon independents.

Let me digress from my odyssey momentarily to explain my usage of the terms "mainstream" and "independent." I've chosen them not only to avoid such heavily loaded labels as conservative and liberal, or intellectual and nonintellectual, or even Liahona and iron-rodder, but because I think the term suggests that the difference between these two types of Mormon lies in the value each puts upon order and liberty. Let me explain.

The church is not monolithic. I don't think it would be accurate, for example, to represent the church population by a single bell curve, with the mainstream clustered in the center. This dromedarian or single-humped view of church demographics gives the false impression that mainstreamers are central and independents are at the fringe. I think the population of the church is better represented by a Bactrian view: two bell curves to the left and right of center, slightly overlapping, with the larger curve, representing mainstream thinkers, to the right and the smaller curve, representing independent thinkers, to the left.

Both groups contain faithful people, reasonable people, and some embarrassing people. Both have their share of agnostics and atheists. What distinguishes one group from the other is that mainstream thinkers believe that spiritual and intellectual growth is more likely to result from a commitment to the values of the church community, while independent thinkers believe that such growth is more likely to result from a commitment to individual spiritual values. Thus mainstreamers see value principally in order, while independents see it principally in liberty.

By the end of the 1970s I realized that I had somehow

landed in the demographic saddle between the humps of this Bactrian camel. Like independent thinkers, I don't trust authoritarianism and value freedom of expression and freedom of conscience. But like mainstream thinkers, I see value in the church community, its ordinances, and in the love and affection that can be found among its members.

In my view, neither of these groups is bad. If anything, they are inevitable. But the difference in their values and orientation makes rivalry and suspicion inevitable, too. With dismay, I have seen the rise of crusading individuals and publications in both camps, the public display of lack of affection between them, and the rise of publicly acknowledged leaders on each side of the line of demarcation.

During the 1980s, this gap has widened as a result of events and stories of events such as the Boyd Packer/Michael Quinn exchange over the writing of Mormon history, the Bruce McConkie/Eugene England exchange over obedience to authority, the William Clayton journals affair, the restructuring of the Church Historical Department, the disagreement over sacred versus secular Mormon history, and the publication of such books as *Mormon Enigma: Emma Hale Smith, America's Saints, The Mormon Corporate Empire, Mormon Polygamy: A History*, and by many of the articles appearing in *Dialogue: A Journal of Mormon Thought* and *Sunstone,* including Margaret Merrill Toscano's "The Missing Rib" (*Sunstone,* July 1985, 16-22).

As the mainstream and independent camps become more defined, there will be, I am afraid, a continuing tendency on the part of each to alienate itself more and more from any truth or good which the other camp has to offer. And, as each side retreats more deeply into its own prejudices, there is an increasing likelihood that tyranny and arrogance will arise in both camps.

In the context of Mormonism, "tyranny" means the use of authority and power to dominate, control, or manipulate others, while "arrogance" is the attitude of self-importance or pride often used to justify power abuses. Tyranny and arrogance are the chief components of oppression, an omnivore that can thrive in a community dedicated to freedom as well as it can in one dedicated to order.

My own struggle with authority—both my lust for it and my aversion to it—has probably made me overly sensitive to oppressive mentalities and activities. This is why I am so worried about the signs of oppression I see appearing in both Mormon camps. Perhaps the most subtle and dangerous of these signs is the failure on the part of leaders in both groups to understand and articulate the limitations of their use of power.

Power is seductive. And leaders, especially religious, moralistic, or humanitarian ones, can be tempted to believe that power is safe in their hands. After all, they're the good guys. That's how I felt in the early 1970s. But I have come to agree with Lord Acton: "Power corrupts, and absolute power corrupts absolutely." This applies to everyone, including church leaders—not only mainstreamers, but independents, too.

A story may illustrate my point. While I was in law school I wrote a class paper called "The Oath and Covenant of the Melchizedek Priesthood." It was about fifty pages long, and I put in 149 notes, quoting biblical scholars and legal sources. Very interesting stuff. For a class paper, I thought it was a *tour de force.* I got a C+. The teacher and I had not gotten along, and I was convinced this grade was his retribution.

I had never confronted a teacher over a grade before; but, as I said, I was a third-year law student and, besides feeling competent, I was also feeling litigious. He physically threw me out of his office after telling me in the clearest possible language that the grade would not be changed. He said that it was not the type of paper called for. I reminded him that the call for papers had been fairly open-ended. Besides, didn't I deserve some credit for creativity. He said that he was the teacher and I was the student, and he would be the judge of that. What's more, he wasn't going to talk about it with me. And moreover, my ideas about priesthood were ludicrous. I retorted that my conclusions were based on research and good evidence. He said that he knew a lot more about priesthood than I did because he had been a high priest for years, had served in a couple of stake presidencies and high councils, and he wasn't going to stand there and listen to me tell him about priesthood. That's when he took me by the arm and shoved me out. I was thinner then.

As his office door slammed behind me, I underwent another paradigm shift. Authority is not a substitute for competence. And competence is not a license to bully. Then, as I wandered off to the Cougareat, I reran the "video" of my life at high speed, trying to recall how often I had abused knowledge or power. Had I been a priesthood tyrant? Had I been an arrogant little twit? The answer was a painful yes. But, thanks to a fine selective memory, I can recall only a few examples of my own rigidity and narrow-mindedness.

Most of these occurred between 1969-73, when I found myself one of the priesthood leaders of the 12th Ward of the BYU 10th Stake. I remember the surge of excitement I felt when I was called to a responsible position in the ward. With the enthusiasm of a Hitler Youth, I whole-heartedly backed the stake's requirement that home teaching visits be done *once a week*. Priesthood leadership meetings were not infrequently held at 6:00 a.m. on weekdays, and I found myself agreeing that young men who did not attend with wide-eyed enthusiasm were unworthy to serve in significant callings. I believed in Zion. We all believed in Zion. It was perhaps the only way in which the idealism of the sixties was allowed to manifest itself at BYU where hard rock, long hair, psychedelic colors, and student protests were thwarted by the administration of President Ernest Wilkinson. Yes, we all believed in Zion. Not bad in itself, perhaps. But we of the 10th Stake were going to build it by complying perfectly—and requiring others to comply perfectly—with the "priesthood correlation program"—the revealed answer to all our problems. Under its aegis, we would march together, arms akimbo and in lock-step synchronization, into the highest glory. It is all too horrible to recall in any greater detail than this.

I have struggled hard to get beyond tyranny and beyond arrogance, not only that of others, but my own as well. I have come to believe that one of the most inspired parts of the Constitution of the United States is the Bill of Rights. I think it should be applied not only in the political sphere but in some sectors of the private sphere, too. But especially in churches. I think we rank-and-file Mormons are morally bound to assert and to exercise with maturity and boldness the inalienable rights of freedom of religion, freedom of speech, freedom of assembly, freedom of the press, and to accord to others and insure for ourselves the rights of due process and equal treatment not only under the law of the land, but of the church as well.

Of course, such notions have only aggravated my personal struggle to find a balance between religious order and liberty. I know now that I don't want to be arrogant or tyrannical and that I don't want to be the subject of tyranny or arrogance either. But I also recognize that I have not yet learned how to escape tyranny while remaining as compliant

MT. LEBANON PUBLIC LIBRARY

as church leaders would like me to be or how always to avoid arrogance while remaining true to my own beliefs. It is the nature of my Mormon experience that has intensified this struggle. I have been troubled to hear of the bishop whose penetrating interrogation into sexual behavior aroused rather than palliated sexual feelings and of the general authority who habitually formed opinions without having any idea of the pertinent evidence or the countervailing points of view. Also disturbing is the story of the stake president who, to the standard requirements for a church position or a temple recommend, added the requirement of a clean-shaven face for men and bras for women. Less known, I suspect, is the account of the high council that excommunicated an individual for committing adultery in the heart.

What concerns me is not that such things happen, but why they happen. I have a theory about how authoritarianism perpetuates itself in the church. Leaders are selected from a rank-and-file who are taught that church leaders are divinely inspired. Not much is said about how such leaders are inspired, and how this inspiration comes, or how it is to be recognized, or how it ought to be put to the test, or how, in some cases, it should be rejected as sheer prejudice. So when one of the rank-and-file suddenly finds himself (or sometimes herself) elevated to some church office, he is likely to imagine that every thought that enters his head, or every action he takes, or doctrine he believes, or every sentimental feeling that washes over him is a manifestation of the divine will. The fewer doubts a leader tends to have about such things, the more apt he is to rely on such "inspiration" regardless of its spirituality, intellectual rigor, or wisdom.

This problem is complicated by the fact that many church leaders are trained to ignore spiritual gifts in people with lesser church status than themselves. Thus, the first counselor will usually feel free to question the ideas of the second counselor, but not the ideas of the bishop, even if the bishop is in outer space. What we have in the church is a spiritual pecking-order, which neatly disposes of the spiritual maturity, experience, and gifts of the rank-and-file.

All this is worsened by our claim to have a lay priesthood in which every worthy male can participate in church administration when, in fact, priesthood authority is under tight hierarchical control and by the fact that the church says very little about the limits of such authority. We have section 121 of the Doctrine and Covenants, but not much elaboration. Members may recognize unrighteous dominion, but they have very few guidelines for defense.

Although I consider myself to have been the victim of an unusually curious list of abuses of ecclesiastical authority (and I can quite easily be persuaded to rehearse a litany of them to any sympathetic audience), I must admit that not all my experiences with the hierarchy have been wretched. With one exception, I think, all the bishops I have known have been kind and spiritual, and have tried hard to be understanding. A bishop in Orem called me as a Gospel Doctrine teacher in spite of opposition from the high priest group leader. Our bishop in Taylorsville called Margaret and me to team teach a class on the Gospel of John in spite of opposition from the stake president who, although he had never met us, had heard some of the old rumors and judged us accordingly.

The problem of tyranny and arrogance in the mainstream camp is, I am sure, matched by the same problem, perhaps more subtly manifest, among independents, where power abuses are more likely to arise as manipulation, cover-up, coercion, character assassination, and the suppression of ideas. Just as mainstreamers can be tempted to think that authority is competence, independents can be tempted to think that their competence is unlimited. Historians, statisticians, scientists, and social scientists—scholars in general—are more apt to make claims rather than disclaimers for their disciplines. They normally do not lay bare the pet peeves, religious biases, and intellectual prejudices that color such endeavors as the choice of a subject to research and analyze, the selection of a thesis or historical question, the data to be included and excluded from a particular treatment, or the choice of tone, of audience, of acceptable and unacceptable hypotheses, or of language and rhetoric to shape and cloak ideas. We are, if possible, even more reticent about divulging our own personal hurts, hostilities, rejections, and failed hopes—all of which may affect our treatment of a given topic.

In my view, scholars are duty bound to state their predispositions and predilections. It is not a particular bias that disqualifies a scholar, but an unwillingness to see it and disclose it. Normally the audience is left to adduce these biases from the grapevine: Did scholar X really once have a falling out with a certain church president? Was scholar Y's grandfather really excommunicated for taking a post-Manifesto polygamous wife even though the marriage was performed by an apostle? Is scholar Z really anti-semitic, or homophobic, or pro-feminist? This information usually has a bearing upon the weight we give to works of scholarship and the light in which we read them. This is so despite the contrary argument that the serious Mormon scholarship being produced today is the product of objectivity and that the conclusions reached therein do not reflect personal and mundane biases, but are conclusions mandated by the facts.

Such nondisclosure amounts, in my opinion, to manipulation or even suppression of important information. I also think it is fair to say that the independent camp sometimes gives short shrift to those who do not approach Mormonism with certain "acceptable" assumptions, methodologies, and conclusions, and who do not express themselves in value neutral rhetoric. A Mormon scholar who deviates from these standards is likely to get something of a chilly reception.

The mainstream, too, can be dishonest or disinformative, especially if it is attempting to sequester data that may prove damaging or embarrassing. When, for example, was the last time anyone heard in general conference a disclosure by the church of its income and expenditures? Today we are treated to a rather curious circumlocution by the auditor that the church uses standard accounting procedures. But never is there a single word uttered about where the money comes from or where it goes—let alone how much there is. The report is remarkable for the absence in it of a single dollar figure. I understand that most businesses keep their financial records private. But I object to this practice when it is employed by the church for it not only tacitly adopts a business practice repugnant to its spiritual mission (and thereby suggests that there is some economic nastiness to be covered-up) but withholds its information from its members while insisting that they, in turn, be fully transparent to the church about their private finances. This one-way transparency is a form of disinformation that shields those in power from accountability for its use.

Apparently neither camp of Mormonism can see the need for a balance between rational and intuitive approaches. Both prefer instead a one-sided orthodoxy predicated on one modality or the other.

Look at the treatment of Joseph Smith. Mainstream thinkers tend to idealize him, while independent thinkers tend to desecrate him. Thus he is depicted in terms of uncreditable panegyric or unedifying exposé.

In visitors' centers, church movies, pamphlets, lesson manuals, and spoken addresses we are presented with Joseph the Unblemished Lamb—the young, pure-minded, religiously-puzzled frontier seeker to whom the Father and the Son appeared and whom they established not only as the head of the dispensation of the fullness of times, but as the ideal son, the ideal brother, the ideal athlete and husband, father and leader. Because the mainstream has adopted Joseph as an ideal role model, his image must remain perfectly smudgeless. He must remain the noble martyr. Any negative assessment of him must be the slander of anti-Mormonism. This is the sanitized Joseph, scrubbed, shampooed, and always clad in a clean white shirt.

In the scholarly journals and histories of independents, however, we find the Joseph of occult beginnings and tantalizing historical gaps and inconsistencies, the glib and persuasive peep-stoner of Palmyra, the money-digging, dowsing huckster with a penchant for plagiarism and a weakness for brass bands and orgasm. This is the debunked Joseph, the product not only of anti-Mormonism, but of some who claim to be writing "objective" Mormon history.

I realize that this is something of an overstatement. I have a weakness, I am told, for overstatement. For the record, I want to say that *all* my overstatement is *always* intentional. I do it to promote the doubtful cause in our closed community of providing a counterweight to both understatement and non-statement. However, my own predilection for this type of expression has not blinded me to the fact that scholars and historians of Mormonism have mostly written moderate portrayals of Joseph Smith. My own use of hyperbole is not meant to deny the existence of the moderate views, but to emphasize that the spectrum is defined by the extremes and that it is the tendency of some individuals to gravitate toward them. So we have Joseph the Sacred—a model to help the mainstream enforce moral order. And then we have Joseph the Profane—an icon to ward off spiritual or ecclesiastical pressure. But these are not true portraits of Joseph. They are caricatures, a litmus test for ascertaining which camp of Mormonism an individual is loyal to. The mainstream is apt to dismiss those who hold less than the idealized view of Joseph as apostates, while the independents are apt to dismiss those who hold more than the debunked view of Joseph as apologists.

Thus the mainstream press cannot deal forthrightly with Joseph's plural marriages, which are an affront to the church's modern view of chastity and morality. On the other hand, the independent Mormon press has not yet convincingly dealt with the spiritual meaning plural marriage may have had for those who introduced it into the church.

I think it is futile to judge Mormonism by the actions or motives of Joseph Smith, who, in my view, was caught between the ordination of the heavens and the permutations of the earth, trapped between the paradoxical demands of his earthly nature and his heavenly visions, between the needs of the individual and of the community, between civilization and the wilderness, between the world and the church, between the Saints and God—the struggling, imperfect prophet in whom God's work was unfinished and through whom God's work remains unfinished.

Perhaps Joseph is not an ideal anything and cannot readily be used to justify either an obsession for moral order and ecclesiastical authority or an obsession for personal freedom and individual competence. Perhaps God, having foreseen that Mormon mainstreamers would develop a fetish for self-righteousness, called, as the founding prophet of the church, a prodigal. Perhaps, having foreseen that Mormon independents would develop a fetish for the urbane, God launched the Restoration through a magician. Seen from this perspective, Joseph is not just a problem to both camps, he is an antidote: a corrective to the idea that Christian salvation is the wages of either human righteousness or human intellect, but that it remains as always the gift of God to all who will, like Joseph Smith, struggle to repent, struggle to forgive, and struggle to bear the crosses of the world.

Earlier I urged scholars, speakers, and writers to disclose their prejudices so that readers and listeners could better judge how they are handling their material. Obviously, it is only fair to reveal my biases.

My strategy for coping with the on-going "crisis" of my faith is not to abandon my beliefs but rather to believe in more and more. This process has been going on for some time. Today I believe in a large and odd assortment of things: I believe in justification by grace and sanctification by the blood of Christ, the literal resurrection from the dead, and the whole of Christian eschatology with Christ coming at the end of the world, red in his apparel.

But when it comes to cosmology, my views are quite unorthodox. People who know me wonder if there is any religious idea I don't believe in. For me, there is but one true way of salvation but many true ways of worship. I believe in the worship of Catholics, Protestants, Jews, and mystics of the East and the West. I have worshipped with many of them and have been edified. I have rejoiced with pagans and have come to respect the skepticism of agnostics and atheists. I may be the last person on earth, except for Margaret, who believes in the Egyptian, Greek, Roman, and Norse gods, in elves and fairies, and angels that bring gold plates. I believe in those, too. I am not bothered by improbabilities. The whole universe appears improbable to me. Yet there it is.

I believe that none of us and that none of our religions has the corner on the truth. We must get truth where we can, even in Masonry and magic. The Lord is at the center of it all. And his glory has seeped into everything. Our calling is to mine it like gold.

I have come to realize that we are all oppressed and that we are all oppressors. At times I fear there is no escape from the jaws of this dilemma. But in my heart I believe there is an escape. Christ has shown us the way. It is the way of the cross.

It comes down to humility—a humility I have never been able to satisfactorily achieve—willingness to accept the good in our rivals and our opposites. The humility of women who, in spite of everything, continue to acknowledge the good in men; of men who, without fear, can acknowledge the power in women. It is a very idealistic notion I am advocating, the notion that the wise must not envy the beautiful nor the beautiful the wise, that the poor must not despise the rich nor the rich the poor, that the high must abase themselves that the low may be exalted. And it must happen not just once, but over and over again, forever.

Envy is the enemy of reconciliation, and I see reconciliation as the only way to close the widening wound in Mormonism. Because I have come to accept the claims of Jesus Christ, I see reconciliation in terms of him alone—in his words, yes; but also in the patterns of his works.

It seems to me that the words of the Old Testament are a witness against tyranny, against the oppression of the powerless by the powerful. It seems to me, too, that the words of the New Testament are a witness against arrogance, against the pride and prudence of the wise.

Christ himself rejected the tyranny and arrogance of both Jews and Greeks. He was a rebuke to both. He opposed both worldly status and worldly wisdom, and the oppression that issues from them. His chief rebuke consisted not in his words, but in his works—in his condescension and crucifixion. For if God had to die to be reconciled to his enemies, must we not do the same?

For me the greatest story in literature has for its hero God himself. It begins: "A certain man has two sons." It is well known. There is the stay-at-home grumbling son who covets wealth and stability, and there is the libertine prodigal who wants his freedom. Their father divides their inheritance between them. When the prodigal has wasted his substance with riotous living and has nothing to eat but pigs' husks and nowhere to go but home, he returns. "But when he was yet a great way off, his father sees him, and has compassion and ran, and falls on his neck, and kisses him" (Luke 15:11-32). His father kills a fatted calf and makes a feast for this son who hoped only for a servant's status. But his elder brother, angry, will not go in. I've served you all these years, he says to his father. I've never sinned. And you never gave me a ring, a robe, or a feast, nor killed the fatted calf for me. But as soon as your whoremongering son comes home, you do it all for him. The father explains: All that I have is thine, just as all that I have is your brother's. Can you not love one another, as I have loved you? Can you not see in each other the good I see in you? Can you not rejoice when the lost is found or the dead returns to life?

I am still trapped between liberty and order, between my desire and my distaste for church authority. My personal struggle is not over. Perhaps it will not be over until my life is over. God willing, it will be over then. But I have concluded at least this: It is only in the marriage of opposites in Christ Jesus that there is freedom and order and repentance, forgiveness, reconciliation, immortality, and eternal life.

If we are to be free, it seems to me, we must let Jesus crucify in us our inflated opinions of ourselves and our inflated expectations of others. I believe this is the only way each of us can finally be healed. It is the only way we can come to accept all that plentitude of good that God has reserved for us in the hands of those whom we have esteemed to be our enemies. Regardless whether we count ourselves in the mainstream or among the independents, if we Mormons are ever to get beyond tyranny and beyond arrogance, it will be only in and through the crucifixion of Jesus Christ—the judge of the oppressor and the advocate of the oppressed.

Chapter Three.

LIBERTY AND JUSTICE FOR ALL

"Liberty and Justice for All" was originally presented as an informal lecture for the Brigham Young University honors program colloquium in February 1987. Each year thereafter, it was updated, rewritten, and redelivered–always informally–until February 1993. The version here is a formal essay drafted from the lecture notes.

I wish to discuss eight values of a free and open community which I believe are not only indispensable, but often underrated or misunderstood. These are: (1) paradox and irony, (2) the rule of law, (3) democracy of the majority, (4) inalienable human rights, (5) the containment of power, (6) the common good, (7) spontaneous order, and (8) the restraint on criminalization.

Paradox and Irony

We are citizens of the modern, western world, at the end of the twentieth century, at the end of the second millennium. And we want it all. We want to be rich, and we want leisure. We want power, and we want privacy. We want technological progress, and we want a clean environment.

39

We want freedom, and we want a well-ordered society. What is not clear to many of us is that these wants are paradoxical and that we can achieve some only at the expense of others. We cannot have a free market that functions within our total control. We cannot have equality and also have privilege. We cannot have freedom and also eliminate indecencies. We cannot have creativity without threatening traditional values. We cannot earn high returns and avoid risk.

Our conflicting desires give rise to many of the palpable tensions of our culture that we cannot relax in spite of all our efforts. This is so because all life and all the disciplines of life are interrelated. This interrelatedness is the source of the paradoxes we encounter in the world. These paradoxes are often manifest to us as insoluble problems arising out of the interplay of such polarities as male and female, passive and active, culture and nature, tradition and progress—even good and evil. These tensions cannot be eliminated without eliminating something essential, something irreplaceable, something of consummate value. In short, they cannot be eliminated without eliminating one or the other of the rival elements that comprise the paradox. Even what may appear to us as merely nominal opposites, such as Republican and Democrat, are often but superficial manifestations of deeper level conflicts that can be stated as questions: Can an economy be free and moral? Can a free people be economically secure? Can social equality be achieved through authoritarianism? Can morality be achieved by the use of force?

Though many such conflicts present themselves to us as polarities, contraries are not always two-sided. They can be many faceted. When they are, we perceive them as *ironies*: The world is full of these:

* The more money we print, the greater the inflation, the less valuable the money, the more money must be printed.

* The more comforts we demand, the greater the supply of technological advancements, the greater the risk to the environment, the greater the risk to our level of comfort.

* The more powerful a nation, the greater its army, the more advanced its weapons, the greater its need for defense, the greater the risk of destruction.

The tensions these ironies embody are, perhaps, even more important than the issues themselves.

Paradox and irony appear to be essential to liberty. For freedom itself seems to arise out of the paradoxical or ironic nature of our being and the tolerance we, as individuals and as communities, demonstrate for the development and expression of the divergent views suggested by the contrarieties of life. Freedom has less to do with arriving at solutions than with struggling with tensions. Freedom is threatened not by problems, but by the denial of paradox and the imposition of the "one, true, final solution." In a free society whose government is of the people, by the people, and for the people, the dogmas of the quiet past will always be seen to be inadequate to the stormy present. Thus, one of the chief characteristics of a free people is the high estimation placed by its members on rival values and on the effort to solve the unsolvable, attain the unattainable, and reforge the orthodox out of paradox. Practically speaking, free and open societies will always be in a state of flux—revisiting traditions and changing rules based on changed interpretations of truth and justice. In short, freedom, paradox, and irony are inseparable.

The Rule of Law

Equally essential and indispensable to a free society is objectivity in the creation of rules of behavior. This concept is expressed as the "rule of law." The idea of the rule of law is that members of a community should be governed by predetermined, fixed rules of behavior rather than by unpredictable, arbitrary fiat. The power of the "rule of law" concept is derived from the fact that, though the general effect of such rules can be known, the specific effect on particular individuals or groups cannot be foreseen nor can such rules be used to foreordain specific outcomes for specific members of the community. An example of such a rule is the 55-mile-an-hour speed limit. Its legislators foresee only the general effect: vehicular speed will be limited to 55 miles per hour—probably with fairly vigorous enforcement. However, it will not be possible to determine the specific effect such a rule will have on public transportation systems, the environment, or traffic patterns either in the densely-populated, compact townships of the northeast or in the sprawling, open spaces of the far west. Because it does not mandate a specific outcome, this rule is a true law, rather than an order or a command, such as a court order requiring a specific defendant to pay a particular fine.

The benefit of the rule of law is that it protects against arbitrariness. It allows individuals to make specific important decisions within predetermined known rules of the game. In fact, game rules are a good example of genuine objective laws. They are predetermined, they apply to all players, and they do not mandate outcomes. The rules are fixed at the start so that the winners and losers cannot be foreknown. In a game played by arbitrary commands, the game is fixed. The rules are not known at the beginning, but the winner is preselected. The rules keep changing to force a certain predetermined outcome. Manipulating the rules undermines the game because it prevents achievement by merit, strategy, or even luck. A fixed game renders all actions pointless because no action will achieve any result other than that willed by those manipulating the ever-changing rules. The will, talents and luck of the players are nullified in favor of the will, talent, and luck of the rule-makers. This is the essence of tyranny.

Democracy of the Majority

The rule of law alone is insufficient to create and maintain an open society. To be truly open, its members must participate in the process of lawmaking. Democracies are limited when they do not allow all adult members to participate equally in the political process. Though most democracies are open societies, this is not always the case. A tyranny of the majority can be as real as a tyranny of the minority. The ancient city states of Greece were governed by limited democracies, as were some of the Italian city states of the Middle Ages. But a democracy limited to the elite is itself limited. It cannot advantage itself of the full range of the experience and knowledge possessed by all its members. This is the recurring problem in all communities in which the many are governed by the few. Eventually ineptitude, inexperience, inbreeding, inability to understand the minute details and operations of the small networks, patterns, and systems that fit together into the larger social fabric expose such communities to destruction, either by conquest from without or by collapse from exhaustion from within.

Democracies of the majority have proved quite successful, over the long term, at structuring and managing complex societies, even if they appear inefficient at mustering a quick consensus to accomplish short-term goals. Oligarchies and dictatorships, while immediately efficient, do not seem capable of coping with the political and economic tensions of complex societies over long periods of time. The strength of a democracy of the majority lies, in part, in the fact that the majority is always in a state of flux. Individuals align themselves differently on different issues. Thus, we might find liberal protestants and Jews aligned in support of the separation of church and state; and conservative Mormons, Protestants, and Catholics aligned against abortion or in favor of the ritual use of peyote by native Americans. This churning of the constituencies comprising the majority increases the larger community's ability to cope with complexity and political tension. It does not eliminate all problems. Large democracies can only function practically through elected representatives. Often the rules that govern the elected bodies (the legislature, the executive, etc.) are undemocratic. It is not unusual to find that elected politicians of a democratic government organize themselves according to quite undemocratic principles. Thus, we see even in the most democratic countries politicians whose power is derived not from the electorate but from seniority, privilege, family, other special interests, or wealth. The tendency is to evolve into democracies of cartels, in which the government draws its authority not from the individual members of society, but from enclaves of privilege. When this occurs, the society that results, though based on the rule of law and on democratic principles, will not be a genuinely open society because the interest of its individual members will not be seen apart from special-interest groups. To prevent this deterioration, a society must be committed to something deeper than rule of law, deeper than democratic principles.

Inalienable Human Rights

The founders of the United States understood that a majority can act as tyrannically as any king. The question, then, was how to govern by rules created by an ever-changing and ever-reconstituting majority while still protecting the interests of the minority—even a minority of one. The answer cannot be found in the processes of democratic elections, or of democratically elected legislatures and executives. Nor can it be found in the due process required by courts. The answer is substantive, not procedural only. It lies in a society's commitment to the sanctity of the individual, to the belief that each individual is endowed, by God or by nature, with certain inalienable rights that cannot be abridged by any sovereign, be it a potentate, a parliament, or the people themselves.

Many of the most important rights appear in the first ten amendments to the Constitution of the United States—the Bill of Rights. The most famous of these rights are the freedom of religion, of conscience, of speech, of the press, of peaceable assembly. Less well-known is the right to due process—the right to notice and hearing before judgment—including a fair trial, by competent evidence, before an impartial judge or jury, with a full opportunity to call, to cross-examine, to rebut witnesses, to contextualize facts, argue law, and obtain an appellate review of the decisions and actions of the lower court. Some individual rights—like the right to privacy, and a woman's right to an abortion in the first trimester of pregnancy, are not articulated in the Bill of Rights, but grow out of judicial decisions. Obviously, some rights are in conflict with others: a woman's right to liberty conflicts with a fetus's right to life; the right to make and rely on private contracts conflicts with the right to have one's debts discharged in bankruptcy; the right of free speech conflicts with the right to bring an action for libel and slander. The question of which are legitimate rights and which are not will never be answered. But an answer is not as important as the debate over the question. The existence of the debate itself and the freedom to participate in it constitute the most important rights of all. The content of our rights is, perhaps, less critical than our belief that such rights exist, and our commitment to an ongoing public dialogue with respect to the nature of those rights.

This is not to denigrate the process of naming and claiming rights not specifically so denominated—the right to dissent, the right to be able to inform ourselves of facts and opinions, the right to express our personhood and individuality in how we behave, speak, dress, arrange our hair, the right to privacy, the right to sexual and other voluntary, consenting, personal relationships, the right to have and rear children, the right to teach them beliefs and values, the right to break away from parents and create a life of our own.

In a free society, these rights are seen to be inalienable from the individual. They are freedoms inseparable from the personhood of each living soul because without them, that personhood would be threatened, diminished, or snuffed out. Because they are not derived from the group or the elite, these attributes of freedom cannot ethically be abridged by either the masses or the leadership.

The Containment of Power

An open society allows its members to participate freely and fully in the process of identifying, testing, accepting, and discarding values and processes of all kinds—religious, domestic, economic, political, social, etc. Among free peoples, this process is conducted in a way that preserves the power and dignity of private persons and, yet, unites them as members of a community within a framework of received but constantly changing perceptions of reality. The rules of such a society maximize the private sphere and minimize the sphere of government control.

An open society's commitment to individual freedoms and rights depends on the regulation of power among the organs of government and the various communities that make up the society. Without such regulation, power will shift in favor of the few and, if unchecked and uncorrected, will result in the erosion of the rights of the powerless and the aggrandizement of the rights of the powerful.

To prevent this, the power of government must first be limited, divided and balanced. It must be limited so that it leaves a large private sector in which individuals may live, believe, think, speak, write, interconnect, and develop. It must be divided so that not all power gravitates to one or another organ of government, where it will eventually corrupt and subvert the ideals of the open society. And power must also be balanced, not just once, but again and again, day after day; if slight adjustments are not constantly made in the balance of power, the balance will not hold.

In the United States, we are committed by the Constitution to a government of limited powers. The limits of the Federal government are set out in Article I, section 8. But from the beginning of our Republic, these limits have been expanded. Few are the decisions of courts or the enactments of Congress that result in limitations on government power. The problem is that there is no quick and easy way to limit governmental actions. If the government oversteps its bounds, an action must be brought, litigated, appealed until a decision is reached that the action of government is unconstitutional. This works, but it is expensive and time-consuming. The idea of a limited government is a powerful one, but the mechanism for achieving it is elusive. Because we believe in a separation of powers, one branch of government cannot reform the procedures of another. Thus, reforming Congress is in the hands of Congress. The executive branch is charged with restraining itself. And, if limits must be set on the courts, the courts must pass judgment on their own procedures. If an ombudsman were created with power to initiate these reforms, the ombudsman's office would soon become more powerful than the government. It would become the government. Then who would limit the ombudsman?

Ultimately, it is the concept of a limited government and the commitment of the community to that concept that works best to enforce limitations. Popular opinion, the popular press, the opinion of intellectuals and celebrities, the perspective of academicians and experts all come into play to correct governmental overreaching. Unfortunately, all this usually happens too late to avert the damage—the Vietnam War, the Watergate scandal, the Iran-Contra affair, the secret nuclear testing done without warning or public consent. But it often comes into play later to expose and correct the imbalance of power that caused the problem. Our belief that government is not all-powerful, all-good, all-knowing, or all-trustworthy and that the word "government" is but a label for the activities of quite fallible individuals like ourselves may be the most effective protection against the worst aspects of an overreaching government. Limitations on government include limitations of jurisdiction and venue of a court, the ripeness, mootness, or standing of a case, limitations created by public hearings and public censure, economic limitations, and the limitations created by community standards, aspirations, and expectations. Other limitations include political infighting, inefficiency, and fear of exposure.

In a free society, however, limitation on power is not

enough. Power must also be divided and balanced. In civics classes, we learn that power is divided among federal, state, and local governments, and balanced among the executive, legislative, and judicial departments of those governments. This is true. The decisions of courts effect the enactments of legislatures. The orders of the executive can be challenged in court. Legislatures can pass laws to close loopholes opened by courts and executives. The balancing process never ends. And, of course, the people themselves may participate in the balancing act. Scientific studies, investigative reports, demonstrations and civil disobedience can all bring pressure on government and the organs of power often for the purpose of resetting the balance. Perhaps, most effective of all are the demands of the ever-shifting majority, itself, which can serve to counter the accretion of power in the hands of the few. At one time the U.S. space program seemed above criticism. But after the explosion that killed seven space shuttle volunteers, public opinion shifted. The space program lost prestige. Its inefficiency and lack of performance exposed it to scrutiny. Its power was questioned, then limited.

The Common Good

Power, in a free society, must not only be limited, divided, and balanced, it must be directed toward the common good. It is difficult to define the common good because it is often confused with the agendas and aspirations of special interest groups. This it is not. The common good is not the good of the government. It is not the good of the majority or of the minority. It is not any specific result or outcome such as improving health care, fighting crime, eliminating poverty, drugs, or improving the environment. Obviously, intelligent legislation along these lines would clearly be beneficial to the society as a whole, but it is not what I mean by the common good.

The common good has to do with process not substance. It has to do with how government works, not what government achieves. The common good is advanced whenever government acts to decrease the disparity between the powerful and the less powerful, when it works to level the playing field for all, to create greater accessibility of information, to enlarge the borders of any dialogue, to increase knowledge and participation in decision-making, in self-definition, and in diminishing the influence of those wielding arbitrary power and seeking to subvert the organs of government to promote or preserve privileges for the few at the expense of the many. The first business of government is to ensure that government itself remains fair, open, even-handed, and uncorrupted by processes that improperly empower special interests.

Spontaneous Order

A free society is an ordered society. But its order arises out of the voluntary arrangements entered into among private individuals or groups. If a free society is to flourish, its order must grow organically out of the multifarious contracts of its citizens, rather than being legislated and mandated by the few. In short, imposed order is inimical to a free people. An open society cannot remain open if it impedes, as a matter of policy, the interchange of skill and knowledge among its members. Thus, it cannot rely only upon the expertise of a small body, even if such experts are indispensable to its survival. The vision of a closed society is limited to the vision of the small clique of authoritarians who lead it. For strength and flexibility, a free society depends upon the knowledge and skill of all its citizens as they go about making private arrangements for themselves, creating thousands of networks—domestic, economic, religious, intellectual, social, etc. The point is that order in a free society is essentially spontaneous, flexible, and self-adjusting, arising out of innumerable interactions of its members under impossibly complex and subtle circumstances. In a closed society the order is imposed, rigid, limited, and usually extrinsic to the nature of the society itself. Eventually, a closed society must either progress by revolutionary convulsions that break open the narrowly defined categories of its leaders, or else it must succumb. The open society, however, can adjust by means of an innumerable succession of paradigm shifts—often painful, often resisted—that will allow the society to adapt to meet both internal and external challenges. In a closed society, the many rely upon the wisdom of the few; in an open society, the many rely upon the wisdom of the many.

This is another way to say that dissent is essential to freedom. Diversity, division, discord are the daily bread of a free people. The closed society despises divergence and seeks to smooth and homogenize, to make the citizens tractable and obedient, suitable for their predetermined assignments within the larger social apparatus. For this reason, the lubricant of a closed society is propaganda, disinformation, and secrecy, while in an open society it is news, information, and open debate.

The Limitation on Criminalization

The fabric of an open society can be unravelled by the power of the majority to criminalize certain actions, omissions, or conditions. In the same way the Nuremburg laws penalized Jewish participation in both private and public sectors of the Third Reich, democracies can make crimes of unpopular behaviors such as the use of alcohol, the practice of polygamy, polyandry, or polygyny, the establishment of home schools, the burning of draft cards in protest of the government, anti-abortion protest, anti-war protest, the leaking of sensitive but not secret government information, the publication of erotic materials, and the like. The majority may even seek to criminalize, not behavior, but mere status or condition: the condition of being gay or lesbian, the condition of being mentally unstable, the condition of being ill with a fearful disease. Adding to the list of crimes is always done in the name of community morals, for the sake of the "common good" if you will. But the problem with such legislation is not its motive, but its adequacy.

In a free society, the mere agreement of the majority that an act or omission should subject a citizen to criminal penalties should not be enough to add to the list of crimes. There must be more. In fact, there is more. Laws are regularly struck down by the supreme courts of states and of the United States because they constitute misguided or inept attempts by the state to create crimes.

Crimes fall into two major categories: *malum in se* crimes and *malum prohibitum* crimes. Crimes that are *malum in se* are criminal because the action or omission involved is, in itself, reprehensible or evil. Crimes that are *malum prohibitum* are criminal only because the action or omission contravenes an interest of the state (such us the requirement to file one's tax return by April 15 or get an extension).

To be a crime, it must at least be demonstrable that the action or omission to be outlawed involves one or more of the following: (1) the use of arbitrary force (such as terrorism, murder, mayhem, rape, ritual or sexual abuse, incest, kidnapping), (2) the perpetration of a material deceit either by falsehoods, disinformation, or fraudulent nondisclosure (such as conducting medical experiments on patients without their informed consent, or insider trading of securities), or (3) the act of trafficking in contraband (smuggling) or a controlled substance whose addictive effect on individuals is deemed by the majority to constitute a grave threat to the fabric of society.

If none of these can be shown, then the state must demonstrate that it has a vital and compelling interest in requiring its citizens either (1) to avoid the activity prohibited (such as demonstrators' blocking a highway during a protest) or (2) to undertake an activity they would otherwise not do (such as registering for the draft). The problem, of course, is establishing the state's vital and compelling interest. Just what does this mean? Does the state have a vital and compelling interest in coercing, under penalty of fine or imprisonment, the compulsory attendance at school of children under age fourteen? Or seat belt use by passengers in motor vehicles? Or crash helmet use by motorcyclists? Or fingerprinting children in gang-infested school districts? Or the rating of TV shows, movies, books, and CDs?

The question of the state's compelling interest is always debatable, and its determination is susceptible to abuse by the majority. It is very often during the process of creating such *malum prohibitum* crimes that the good, plain people of any community are tempted, for the sake of preserving morality, decency, economic equality, to abuse the power of the state. For this reason, communities often find themselves groping through a briar patch of conflicting philosophies, political ideologies, and special interests. There appear to be no clear, fixed rules on how to make good rules. However, there are some general guidelines that can apply:

* Before creating a criminal statue, other, less drastic options should be considered first. For example, rather than create a law that defines a crime punishable by the state such as a fine for selling indecent materials, it is possible instead to create a civil cause

of action—a tort or an action for breach of contract—
that can serve as the basis for a private law suit
brought by an aggrieved plaintiff against the perpetrating defendant.

* If no other options exist, and a criminal statute
must be enacted, it should be one that does not
inadvertently encourage the police to violate
human rights in the process of gathering evidence
for the prosecution—which would happen if the
state were to criminalize nudity, adultery, or fornica-
tion.

* If a criminal statute must be enacted, it should—like
all other laws—apply to all similarly situated members of the society. A law that prohibits mail fraud
should not have exceptions for the politicians making the laws. To do so would be to favor incum-
bents over challengers in elections. Moreover, laws
should be reciprocal with respect to the powerful
and the powerless. If courts are empowered to hold
people in "contempt of court" for in-court demonstrations of lack of respect, judges themselves
should be chargeable for "contempt of the people"
if they manifest in-court disrespect to the persons
who appear before them.

* If a criminal statute is enacted, it should be applied
even-handedly, not against any particular group or
individuals. It should not be possible to foresee
which specific individuals will be affected by the law
or how precisely that impact will be felt on each.

* Criminal laws should not be passed either to promote or proscribe any ideology.

* Criminal laws should not be passed for the purpose of outlawing a human condition or characteristic, a sexual preference, an illness, a desire, fear, hope, or any scientific, intellectual, artistic, or spiritual assumption, expectation, aspiration, or communication.

Conclusion

Any society dedicated to both liberty and justice for all must necessarily be involved in tension and conflict. There will be no fixed and certain answers, but over time there will emerge from the experience of its members a set of values—procedures, expectations, traditions—for preserving liberty without sacrificing order and preserving order without sacrificing liberty. Some of these values will be embodied in writings, others will not, some will consist of assumptions that run so deep they remain imperceptible or defy precise definition.

The chief business of a free society is to preserve its freedom. To do this it must repeatedly re-examine its received traditions, recall its original aspirations, examine its expectations, challenge its aspirations, question every use of power, create new and preserve old ways of ensuring a level playing field for all.

Order achieved at the expense of liberty is tyranny. Liberty achieved at the expense of order is discord. Justice without liberty is not just. Liberty without justice is not free. For a free and just society to cohere and endure, its citizens must work everyday to preserve the paradox that gives it life.

Everyday they must rededicate themselves again and again to liberty and justice for all.

Chapter Four.

A PLEA TO THE LEADERSHIP
OF THE CHURCH

*"A Plea to the Leadership of the Church" was originally
presented at the Sunstone Theological Symposium in August 1989.*

One of the ironies of my life is that I decided in 1963 to leave
the Catholic church as it was becoming more open to join
the Mormon church as it was becoming more closed. This
irony has been brought home to me repeatedly during the
past several general conferences. We have been told again
and again by prominent general authorities that members
who think or discuss unapproved or controversial religious
ideas or who disagree with or dissent from the official church
position, whether individually or in groups, are being contentious and should not be encouraged by church leaders at
any level. We have also been told that criticism of leadership,
however valuable in a secular context, is not to be tolerated
within the church where leaders are chosen by God, speak
for him, and can be trusted over alternate voices to impart
the truth about doctrine, church governance, and the way to
live in order to obtain the rewards of the celestial kingdom.

As I have listened to and later read these messages, I have
concluded that the cumulative effect—whatever the individ-

ual motives—is to facilitate the exercise over the Saints of the very control, compulsion, and unrighteous dominion God forbids in church revelations (see D&C 121). In fact I felt more and more convinced that such ideas must be corrected or at least questioned. So I began making notes for this essay. As I did so I thought at first that I should address myself to all Mormons. For we are all—and I especially include myself—subject to the subtle, dangerous, and widespread temptation to control, coerce, manipulate, dominate, and compel others. But as I considered again the statements made in general conferences, I decided to address my remarks specifically to the Brethren—the general authorities of the church—as a group (since they act in concert), rather than as individuals. In doing this I speak principally for myself and possibly for those who feel as I do.

Brethren, I assume that my words will somehow be brought to your attention and that you will eventually read this plea. I know it is unusual for a lay member of the church to address you directly in public. I understand too that you may feel I am being presumptuous, inappropriate, and impertinent—though I do not wish to be. You may even be tempted to discipline me. Or you may decide to ignore me and relegate me to the ranks of those whose "basket shall not be full" and whose houses and barns "shall perish" (D&C 121:20). I fervently hope, Brethren, that you will do none of these things—even if what I say wounds your feelings or embarrasses you or causes you to feel anger. Please try to accept that I and others have had our feelings hurt by you, have been embarrassed by you, have been angered by you. Yet in spite of this, we continue to listen to you. Please listen in return. The time has come for us to stop talking past one another and to communicate directly with one another.

I am also aware, Brethren, that you are likely to brand these remarks, or even my desire to be heard, as contentious. Contention, you have repeatedly warned, is of the devil and should be avoided. But this is not really true; contention is not always evil. The apostle Paul writes, "at Philippi, we were bold . . . to speak unto you the gospel of God with much contention" (1 Thess. 2:2). The scripture says that Michael the archangel contended with the devil over the body of Moses (Jude 1:9). To Isaiah the Lord said, "I will contend with him that contendeth with thee, and I will save thy children" (49:25). And in Doctrine and Covenants 90:36 we read: "I, the Lord, will contend with Zion, and plead with her strong ones, and chasten her until she overcomes and is clean before me."

Contention is not evil if it means to plead, to argue, to bring forth strong reasons, or simply to contradict. This type of contention is an inevitable part of growth, of working through differences, of approaching harmony and truth. What the scriptures condemn as contention is not verbal disputation but physical violence or the creation of schisms in the church. In the Book of Mormon, "contention" usually means an armed skirmish or battle. We are told, for example, that Alma and "his guards, contended with the guards of the king of the Lamanites until he slew and drove them back" (Alma 2:33). Here contention means "combat" not argument. This is why it is so often coupled with "war," as in "wars and contentions" (48:20). Jesus warns against the outbreak of such contention—or "conflict"—as a result of doctrinal disputes (3 Ne. 11:28-30). Doctrinal disputes should not lead to violence or divisions in the church. The point of Jesus' teaching is that even if we cannot agree on doctrine or on the interpretation of scripture or on church policy or governance, we can at least avoid renouncing or rejecting or alienating those who disagree with us.

Contention aimed at uncovering truth or struggling toward unity is good, just as constructive criticism is good. It may involve hard words and emotions and may necessitate cooling-off periods, but its purpose is benevolent. Contention aimed at dividing the church, at renouncing and rejecting as evil those who disagree with us, at rendering our opponents powerless, at dismissing them as inferior or worthless, or at inciting people to violent acts is not good, just as destructive criticism is not good. No matter how calmly and courteously it is advanced, its purpose is malevolent.

Brethren, before you judge those you think are contentious, ask yourselves if you are not also contentious. Who has divided the church into leaders and followers, intellectuals and mainstream members, believers and liberals, true voices and alternate voices, active Mormons and inactive Mormons? To label, renounce, stigmatize, or reject your fellow Saints because we disagree with you or cannot accept all you want us to accept is the kind of contention and divisiveness Jesus warned against. And not Jesus only. Joseph Smith said: "I will give you one of the Keys of the mysteries of the Kingdom. It is an eternal principle, that has existed with God from all eternity: That man who rises up to condemn others, finding fault with the Church, saying that they are out of the way, while he himself is righteous, then know assuredly, that that man is on the high road to apostasy; and if he does not repent, will apostatize, as God lives" (in Joseph Fielding Smith, comp., *Teachings of the Prophet Joseph Smith* [Salt Lake City: Deseret Book Co., 1964], 156). This famous statement, made by the prophet on 2 July 1839, is often quoted to members who are critical of you as a warning that criticism can lead to apostasy. But this twists the original meaning and purpose of the statement. Joseph Smith did not say these words to church members who were critical of their leaders.

He said them to church leaders—to apostles and seventies—who were critical of church members. He warned leaders of the church not to put themselves above others, not to condemn others, not to find fault with the church, not to say that members are out of the way while leaders are righteous.

Brethren, you ignore this warning whenever you create, maintain, or reinforce categories of church membership or attempt to classify people as intellectuals, liberals, or dissidents. We all do it whenever we believe there are people less valuable than ourselves, whose voices we do not have to hear—people who must listen to us but who have no right to be heard. We violate Joseph Smith's warning whenever we insist on the use of titles to distinguish leaders from followers. Did not Jesus instruct us not to call each other by titles? We are brothers and sisters, children of Christ. We are equals and our relationship to one another arises out of love not power. This is true even of our relationship to God, to whom we pray not by any title but in the name or by the name of Jesus.

We have been told to esteem our brothers and sisters as ourselves. This type of equality lies at the heart of the golden rule. Unfortunately, my experience in the church causes me to wonder: Do you Brethren believe the golden rule applies to you? Do you treat others as you would wish to be treated? Do you accord others the scope and privileges you claim for yourselves?

Brethren, please do not avoid these questions and admonitions simply because they may be couched in critical terms. Jesus did not put himself above his critics. Is it not a form of tyranny for you to forbid us from complaining about the quality of your leadership? Yes, we should not speak evil of you falsely. In fact we should not speak evil falsely of anyone. But I believe I have not spoken falsely of you—even if I have spoken bluntly. My criticism is meant to help rather than to harm you. In spite of this, I know that some may feel that these remarks are damaging to my faith and to the faith of others. After all, you will say, if all this needed saying, we have a prophet to say it. The Lord would speak through his prophet and not suffer us to be led astray. But, Brethren, this only means that the Lord has promised to remove a prophet who attempts to lead the church astray. It does not mean that we cannot go astray on our own without being led. It does not mean that church leaders are always right and on the right course. It does not mean that we can be complacent, that we can simply turn the church over to a few men and never worry about it again. It does not mean that our leaders are above making mistakes and falling into errors and temptations. Prophets can be and have been wrong. Though Aaron was called by God, was it not he who built the golden calf? Did not Moses also make mistakes? He not only murdered an Egyptian and sought to govern Israel as an autocrat, but was later forbidden to enter the promised land because he and Aaron had failed to trust God in the wilderness of Zin (Num. 20:12; 27:13). Remember too that Peter, the chief apostle, not only denied Christ three times but could not find the courage to send the gospel to the gentiles for nearly twenty years after the Lord had told him to do so. Eventually the Holy Spirit, no longer willing to endure the intransigence of the church leadership, set apart Paul and Barnabas to commence this work. More recently Spencer W. Kimball and other general authorities failed to recognize that the "Salamander Letter," the Joseph Smith III Blessing, and several other historical documents were forged.

My point is simply that prophets do not always speak as prophets. They can be wrong. This means that you cannot lay claim to infallibility. Nor can you forbid members from criticizing you, for that is tyranny. Nor can you claim superior spirituality or righteousness, for that is the kind of arrogance against which Joseph Smith warned. Nor can you claim to be those whom God will speak to first about important religious doctrines. When it came to the resurrection of the dead, Jesus announced it first not to those who were the acknowledged leaders but to women. This does not mean that you are not true prophets, only that you cannot claim to be unerring or preeminent among the Saints.

What you *can* claim is responsibility for watching over the flock of God, not as "lords over God's heritage, but as examples to the flock" (1 Pet. 5:3). You can be first in love, first to teach the gospel, first to reveal the ordinances of salvation and exaltation, first in the spiritual gifts, first to make open disclosure, first to confess sin, first to admit pride, first to hold out hope of salvation for the oppressed, the helpless, the weak, and the lost.

This is not the Church of Jesus Christ of Latter-day Leaders. It is the Church of Jesus Christ of Latter-day Saints. The leadership of the church is not the church. It is an important part of the church—even an indispensable part. But so are the Saints. The scripture says that the head should not say to the foot, "I have no need of thee." But this is what the church institution says every time it asserts that leaders are more important, more valuable than non-leaders. It is the message we get from the way the church functions: leaders sit in council, preach in conference, lay down rules, while we members are there to soak it all up—and if we do this long enough and well enough, then perhaps we too, if we have been prudent and wise and male, may become leaders.

But the church should not be divided in this way. It should be a community of believers, a repository of spiritual gifts, where we rely on each other. When you do not rely on the spiritual gifts of members, you effectively deny those gifts. You do not deny their existence, of course, but you deny their operation as the driving force of the church. This happens when you refuse to accept the operations of the spirit that lie outside your control, as they are manifest among the members in their work places, in their study groups, and in their forums and symposiums too. It happens when you reject the spirit as it shines through the unofficial publications to which members contribute.

The revelations teach that anyone who speaks when moved upon by the Holy Ghost speaks the mind and will of the Lord (D&C 68). This means that revelation does not come solely to those who sit in the church's highest councils but to those who meet together to comfort one another, support one another, love one another. Jesus said that where two or more are gathered in his name, he is in their midst (Matt. 18-20). He did not say that he would be only with two or more of the priesthood or of the righteous or of the mainstream. His statement is unqualified. People who gather in Christ's name are the people of Christ. This is the church in its most comprehensive sense. It may not be the divinely authorized church institution. But it is the Church of Jesus Christ, in any case, because he is in the midst of it. If this is so then Christ is with those of us who attend the Sunstone symposium in spite of our struggles, our doubts, our questions, and our sins. He is with us every bit as much as he is with you Brethren in your councils, in spite of your struggles, your doubts, your questions, and your sins. And if God is for us, who can be against us? Who can say to the people of Christ, "You should not meet together or speak or question"? Such a prohibition seeks both to rob us of our freedom of conscience, of religion, of speech, and of peaceable assembly—rights vouchsafed to us by God through men and women raised up and inspired for this very purpose—and it seeks to deny us the exercise of our spiritual gifts, whose existence and expression are crucial to the vitality of the church. As a friend of mine says, baptism washes away our sins not our rights. Nor in my view does it wash away our doubts, our questions, or our concerns. To proscribe such rights and blessings is to deny the power of God manifest in ordinary members.

Though the distinction between leader and member may help us to see our different functions in the body of Christ, they should not be used to determine our individual value to God or to the church. We are each equally valuable to God. And the value of each of us has been set by God in the person of Jesus Christ. He died for each of us. This means that each mortal is as valuable as God himself. We must deal with others as if each person were as valuable as our own person, as valuable as the person of God. This does not mean that we are to pretend to be equal in experience, understanding, wisdom, authority, health, agility, intelligence, or talents and gifts. But it does mean we are equal in value and dignity. No person, no matter how powerful, should treat another person, no matter how weak, any differently than he or she would be treated, any differently than she or he would treat someone he or she values and respects.

In my view the key to understanding Christ's admonitions about human relationships is to understand this concept of mutual and reciprocal esteem and dignity. Brethren, this means that it is not enough for you to say that you love us. People love their pets. They love their property. They love their slaves. What Christ requires of us is that we love each other as equals. He said, "A new commandment I give unto you that you should love one another as I have loved you. By this shall all men know that you are my disciples, if you have love one for another" (John 13:33-34).

How did Christ love us? He made himself equal to us, so that we could be made equal to him. The problem with us is that we are not equal. We are not equal in earthly things, so how can we expect to be equal in heavenly things? The gospel is the supreme message of mutual, reciprocal, symmetrical, divine love. The greatest makes himself or herself equal to the lowliest. Eve did this. Adam did this. Christ did this. Christ poured out his life for the least of his creations. He was despised and rejected, a man of sorrows and acquainted with grief. He bore our iniquities and chastisement. With his stripes we are healed. He asks us to love one another as he loved us—not counting himself more valuable than the least of us but esteeming the least of us as worthy to die for.

Brethren, do you love us as Christ loves us? Yes, you do love us. But too often there are strings attached to that love. I know you will be tempted to dismiss my words because of what you may call my "anger." But anger is not evil unless it is coupled with the desire or intent to do harm. My anger and the anger of other loyal Mormons is not motivated by hostility but by grief, sorrow, depression, helplessness. Our anger flares sometimes because it makes us feel less helpless and overwhelmed. But you must understand that both our anger and our depression are the same. They are both manifestations of our fear.

What are we afraid of? To tell the truth, Brethren, many of us members are afraid of you, afraid that we will never be acceptable to you no matter what we think or say or do, no matter what we suffer or how deeply we believe. We are afraid you will never accept us or our sacrifices because they are not the ones you want. In other words we fear your conditional love. We want you to love us unconditionally. But you seem so reluctant to do this. The message of your conditional love is in nearly every speech you give. In our hearts we know that we can never meet all your conditions, all your standards, and also be true to our own spiritual experiences. We are afraid because we have been made to carry the burden of your narrow assumptions and inflated expectations. Believe me, Brethren, there are many who feel this way. Our anger rages quietly beneath a veneer of obedience and respectability. I believe Joseph Smith when he said, "There is one thing under the sun that I have learned and that is that the righteousness of man is sin, because it exacteth over much; nevertheless, the righteousness of God is just, because it exacteth nothing at all, but sendeth the rain on the just and the unjust, seed time and harvest, for all of which man is ungrateful" (Smith, *Teachings of the Prophet Joseph Smith*, 317). Brethren, we are afraid because we feel that too often you have preached and imposed not the righteousness of God but your own righteousness.

Why must you exact from us "over much"? Why do you not love us unconditionally? Why will you not attend our gatherings and symposiums? We do not want to attack you or ask you to endorse us. We need your love just as you need ours. Why divide us from you on the basis of who is in charge or who is right? Neither righteousness nor rightness nor authority can serve as the unifying principle of the church. The Pharisees believed that the people of God could be united on the principle of purity and righteousness, but this view led to elitism and intolerance. Catholics insisted that all Christians unite around the authority of the Bishop of Rome, but this created the split between the Roman and Orthodox church. Protestants insisted that Christians unite around the right interpretation of scripture, but this only resulted in a scandal of schisms. Must we make the same mistakes? Christ revealed that the true unifying principle of the church is charity.

Though we have the gift of prophecy and understand all mysteries and all knowledge and though we have all faith so that we could remove mountains, without charity we are nothing. We could give everything to the poor, but without charity it is an empty gesture. Charity is patient and kind, it does not envy, it does not strut or boast. It is not rude, self-serving, easily provoked, threatening, or malicious. Charity gives us unity and covers us. Brethren, no matter how we may disagree on doctrine, no matter how we may struggle with power and authority, we are one body. This means that in spite of our differences, we must love one another and hang on to one another and resist the temptation to renounce, reject, or alienate one another.

You may ask: Shall we not excommunicate dissidents and apostates? My answer is that if it can be proved by good evidence that someone is deliberately, willfully, and maliciously seeking to do palpable injury to a church member, to church property, or to specifically defined relationships to which members or church institutions are a party, then excommunication *may* be appropriate. But it is clearly wrong to oust or punish members just because they dissent or disagree. The church is no longer an infant. It has survived and will continue to survive differences of opinion.

Besides, we all make mistakes. We all disobey. We all are sinners. The church is a hospital for sinners. It is not a museum for saints. You Brethren should not expect people to be perfect before you give them your love. We must love each other first, so that we can have the strength and courage to be made perfect. Some of you Brethren may not like this idea. You may feel it is not fair for sinners to be loved in the same way as the righteous. You are not happy that those who have labored eight hours get the same wage as those who worked only for a half an hour. So you are keen to create justice. You want to punish sinners so that they understand the gravity of their sins, so they know they cannot have the fun of sinning and then the reward of righteousness. But people who sin and recognize their sins know already that sin is not fun—it is terrible. Most of them are crying for a way out. Those who do not understand the awfulness of sin are the self-deceived, the self-righteous, and the deranged.

Please do not misunderstand me. I am not saying that criminals should not be punished according to just laws and due process. But why punish sinners who are not criminals? Their sin is their punishment. Why not accept that Jesus was punished for our sins and leave it at that? The great judgment has already taken place on Golgotha. Continuing judgment can only alienate people seeking God's grace. Unity in spirit comes only through loving one another in spite of our sins. True we must all repent. But what we must repent of most is the sin of withholding our love from people we do not approve of. Of course we cannot be saved in our sins. But we can be loved in our sins and we can love in our sins. God who is sinless loved us while we were yet sinners. He loved the sinful world so much that he sent his own son into it to establish that each sinner is as valuable to God as Jesus Christ himself.

Brethren, why have you been so harsh with your conditional love? Never has the church had more obedient, faithful, tithe-paying members. Never have you had more respect, prestige, and power to do good. Why then do you not appear to be satisfied? You have been told that it is the weak things of the earth that shall break down the mighty. Can you not then rejoice in our weaknesses? Do you not realize that our weaknesses and our strengths are the same? It is our intelligence that makes us question. It is our love of freedom that makes us unmanageable. It is our passion that leads us to sin. It is our yearning for something beyond this world that makes us indifferent sometimes to convention. God has given us these weaknesses to make us humble. Why deplore them? Why despise us?

You seem not to trust us. But you want us to trust you. You want us to trust the bishops, stake presidents, mission presidents, and other leaders you have chosen. You want us to believe that you could and would do no wrong. If ever there is a dispute between a member and a leader, you believe that it is the leader who is right. But the truth is that you leaders are really no better than we Saints. But you seem not to accept this. And you continue to treat us as if we had no stake in the church at all.

Why do you hide information from us? Why do you keep from us the books and records of your dealings and minutes of your councils? Why do you tell us only those facts that make you look good? Why do you tell us only the success stories? Why do you not show us the liability side of your ledgers? Why do you refuse to tell us how much money the church has, how it is spent, and the nature and amount of losses and gains? How can you expect us to be open with you about our lives and finances, when you are not open with us about yours?

Why does the church have to have so much money? So much land? So much invested with the world? Is it because of your fear? Do you want the temporal power and influence of the church to shield us from the reproach of the world, to prove to our detractors that we are worthy of their praise? We were persecuted and driven out of seven states. Do you want to make sure it does not happen again? Is this why you want money in the bank, realty free and clear, stores of supplies, and friends in Washington, D.C.? But is it good to have so much of a stake in this world? Was it not God who allowed us to be persecuted? He could have stopped it. He can start it up again at any time. His chastisement could have made us pure had we accepted it. But it hurt so much that we have vowed never to let it happen again. Because of the pain of the past, you seem determined to cut us off from our history, from Joseph Smith, from the nineteenth century with all of its doctrines and doings. You seem determined that we should assimilate completely into our modern American culture. I doubt that we have ever truly healed from the wounds of persecution, truly forgiven our persecutors, or truly forgiven our God for allowing these abuses to befall us.

Brethren, neither you nor we are blameless in this. We have all been too anxious to succeed in worldly terms. You should have corrected us. Instead you seem to promote our worldly success because you believe it reinforces the good image of the church. But a church with a good image is not the same as a good church. Your emphasis on earthly achievements, your infatuation with power, the fact that you see money as a sign of spiritual election, the church as a business, yourselves as its board of directors, and its product as a respected and respectable people—these are all signs of bad judgment. I know you do not like to have your judgment questioned. You like to think your judgment is the judgment of God. But it is not. You are flesh and blood like we are. And we have been told not to trust in the arm of flesh—even your flesh.

You may be thinking that I am ungrateful, that I do not understand the sacrifices you make and have made as general authorities, including the toll these callings have taken on your personal lives, your families, your opportunities, your personal wealth. After all, you say, "Why blame us? We didn't call ourselves." No, you did not call yourselves and, yes, you have made sacrifices for the church. You have sacrificed a great deal—but not your power, or your status, or your respectability. You project an image of yourselves as men who are perfect, while we are imperfect. You call the Saints to account, even publicly, but you rarely call each other to account and never publicly. You admit no mistakes. You seem never to repent. And you are not known to forgive often. You seem unable to accept the fact that you cause some of us pain. And you are tempted to punish those of us who cry out.

You yearly deliver patriotic speeches, but you do not provide any means whereby we may express our dissent. You do not take seriously or accept alternate voices. You do not let us participate in church governance unless we have been carefully screened and correlated. Nor do you account to us for your stewardships. You do not believe the high are accountable to the low. But Jesus did not teach this. He made himself accountable to his creations. He let himself be judged before he would judge.

The truth is that you are as afraid of us as some of us are of you. You think we will despise you because you are not perfect prophets, just as we fear that you will despise us because we are not perfect Saints. So we hide behind a cloak of activity and respectability, while you hide behind walls of granite and move about in underground tunnels.

These are the signs of mutual fear not mutual love. This situation is our fault as much as it is yours. It is our fault that you are afraid to be real, personal, human. We have made you unapproachable. We have done this by sinning against you. Our sin is that we do not love you unconditionally. We expect you to be perfect, to always have the right answers, to never make a slip. If ever you do we lose our testimonies and make you feel responsible. But you are not responsible for what we believe, say, or do. You are only responsible for what you believe, say, or do. You should call us to account for our conditional love, even as I call you to account for yours.

Brethren, please, do not hide, do not threaten, do not punish, do not breathe out cursings. Do not hold secret councils or keep secret files. Do not look for scapegoats or resort to the silent treatment. Do not exercise control, compulsion, or unrighteous dominion. These are not answers. The answer to our mutual dilemma of conditional love is for all of us to repent, to forgive, and to love one another as Christ loves us. God is humble and meek. We know this because on the cross he showed us that he deals with us out of the divine weakness of love rather than out of the earthly strength of power. He wants us to be humble and meek too. To be humble is not to be subservient. It is to be unimpressed with oneself, one's calling, one's achievements, one's image, one's power, one's career, and one's future. To be meek is to see ourselves as we really are without our masks of respectability, infallibility, invulnerability, invincibility. But we are not meek. We are not humble. And you Brethren are partly responsible because you have not made these things clear.

My advice, Brethren, is this: Choose love not power. Do not hide behind your authority or your masks of solemnity, severity, and composure. Do not cling to your privacy. It is not healthy for you to have both power and privacy. Lay aside worldly prudence and wisdom. Do not group think. Do not group speak. Do not repress your best spiritual instincts in order to be good team players. Do not calculate so much or rely so much on statistics. Do not flatter or succumb to flattery. Reveal yourselves. Do not be ashamed. His grace is sufficient to cover you. And especially do not be ashamed that your revelations and contacts with God are no better or more frequent than our own. Do not be afraid of women or of their claims. Recognize that they are your equals in every way. Do not clone yourselves by picking leaders who are identical to you in the way they think, speak, dress, and view the world. Do not concern yourselves with being respected or respectable. These are not the same as holiness. True religion has never been respectable. If you are laughed at, laugh along. If you are criticized, search your souls.

Jesus did not say, "count my sheep." He said, "feed my sheep." Do not shun the needy, the weak, the oppressed. Love the wretched, the idle, those who are not like you. Exalt the poor. Live with them. Give away more. You need not agonize over whether the resources of the church will be exhausted by all the poor, the irresponsible, the unwashed. The earth is the Lord's and the fullness thereof. He will provide. Be generous and you will find your baskets full of fish and loaves and grain, and hidden in the grain will be gold besides. Do not be afraid of the unworthy. They are more like you than you think. Remember if your enemy asks for your cloak, give her your coat also. If he wants you to go a mile, go with him two miles. Do not think about what you will eat or wear or how your families will be provided for. Consider the lilies of the field, how they grow, they toil not neither do they spin. Yet Solomon, in all his glory, was not arrayed as one of these. These words, as you know, were not spoken to all the disciples, but they were spoken to the twelve, to the seventy. Accept them.

Brethren, you possess the keys of the kingdom. They were given to you to hold in trust for us, not only for the Saints of the church but for the people of the Lord every-where. Use them for our sakes. With them open the doors of your councils. Open the archives of the past. Open the records of your dealings. Open the treasuries of the church.

Open the scriptures and expound them. Open your mouths in blessings. Open your hands in generosity. Open your eyes. Open your ears. Open your minds. And above all open your hearts.

I have been both blunt and bold, but I am not without respect. That I have addressed you directly means that I hope you will receive bravely what I have said without rancor. With God's grace we can all begin to appreciate each other's differences, accept them, even celebrate them, and, without obliterating them, transcend them. It is not too late to rid ourselves of narcissism, elitism, exclusivity, superficiality, rigidity, pride, authoritarianism, self-righteousness, and fear. The church will not be overthrown by the revelation of our weaknesses. It will be strengthened by it. The weak through love shall conquer the strong. The church will endure. It is not too late to make the church a refuge, a "safe place," where every Saint is a leader and every leader is a saint, a place where we may all put off our masks of pretense and live in openness, in vulnerability, in health, in wholeness, in peace. This is the end and purpose of the gospel of Jesus Christ and its restoration through Joseph Smith.

Why then should we tarry? Let us get on with what must be done. Let us repent and forgive. Let us be fearless. Let us be full of faith, hope, and charity. And let us ever bear in our hearts the conviction that if we will but love all people without pretense, without fear, without condition, with perfect, symmetrical, and reciprocal esteem, the church will never fail. And the gates of hell will not prevail against us.

Chapter Five.

THE CALL OF
MORMON FEMINISM

"The Call of Mormon Feminism" is a single essay that combines two speeches dealing with feminist issues. The first, a short speech entitled "The Call of Mormon Feminism" given as part of a panel presentation at the Mormon Women's Forum on 30 November 1988, comprises the first section of the essay. The second speech, first presented on 7 September 1991 in response to Rodney Turner as part of a panel discussion on "How Shall We Worship God the Mother?" comprises the second section of the essay entitled "The Worship of the Lady."

Imbedded in the Restoration movement is the doctrine that women in every way are the equals of men. I believe that Joseph Smith was the source of this doctrine and, therefore, the first exponent of Mormon feminism. It was he who gave the stamp of approval to the organization of the Female Relief Society of Nauvoo. It was he who told its earliest members that he intended to make of that society a "kingdom of priests." It was he who promised its members that they would obtain the blessing of the priesthood, with the right to heal the sick and cast out devils, and that they would come into possession of all the privileges enjoyed by male priesthood holders.

Since those early days Mormon feminism has fended for itself, living on its own, within the culture of the Latter-day Saints, most often surviving in obscurity in the hearts of numerous women and men.

The resurgence of Mormon feminism has occurred, I believe, in response to certain troubling conditions in the modern church. The most obvious of which include the disenfranchisement of women from the priesthood and the exclusion of women from church governance. But the problems caused by patriarchal authoritarianism have wreaked more damage than this. They have led to a larger and growing spiritual malaise that is marked by a lack of inner life—a sense that we have somehow strayed from our religious mission, that we have borrowed too much from the male world of business and commerce, that we have become too narrow, too elitist, too self-righteous, too legalistic and judgmental, and that we are adrift in dark seas.

Because the feminist view seeks to respond to these concerns, it involves much more than a demand for equality in Mormon culture. It is more than a claim for power in the ecclesiastical or priestly hierarchy. It is more than a plea for cultural and social change. Mormon feminism, I believe, is a call to repentance—a call for the fundamental spiritual revitalization of our entire religion. For this reason, its goals lie at the heart of the gospel of Jesus Christ. Mormon feminism asks us not only to believe in, but to conduct our lives and our ecclesiastical affairs on the premises that God's love is truly without bounds or conditions, that God is truly no respecter of persons, that God called the sexes, the families, the societies, and the nations of the earth to be one through the blood of Jesus Christ, and that therefore men and women are truly spiritual equals in God's sight. What I hear in the voices of the exponents of Mormon feminism is a call to all Mormons—male and female—to reject the primacy of male-dominated institutional power and to embrace instead the powers of the spirit under conditions where men and women share equal responsibility for the welfare and governance of the church.

The intent of Mormon feminism is not to create a new religion, but to stop Mormonism's steady and appalling slurge away from the spirituality and egalitarianism of the restored gospel and toward the materialism, corporatism, and elitism that characterize the modern world. The feminist movement is not, therefore, an apostate movement, but a movement to counter apostasy. It calls for spiritual renewal. And for this reason it is necessarily involved, at least at first, in the process of reexamining and reinterpreting scripture and doctrine. It asks us to re-read all the books, to see where we have gone wrong, to understand where we have become entangled in false traditions and false philosophies.

The initial task of Mormon feminism involves the development of a new way of seeing—a new hermeneutical approach—that attempts to purify our way of looking at our standard works so that we no longer rely upon them as authorizations for oppression. Though the feminist view will undoubtedly continue to focus on the problems and sufferings of women under patriarchy, its ultimate concerns will necessarily extend beyond these immediate afflictions to embrace ideas that tend both to reform and reaffirm important aspects of our religion. The new feminism seeks to reaffirm our fundamental faith in the gospel of Jesus Christ—justification by the spirit, sanctification by God's blood, the

MT. LEBANON PUBLIC LIBRARY

resurrection of the flesh, and our ultimate deification. But it also seeks to reform our views so that we see again, in a purer light, many of our most treasured teachings.

Without losing our grasp on Christ crucified and risen, the feminism I accept asks us to acknowledge the limitations of authoritarianism and hierarchy and to accept the concept of a democratized priesthood in which members are valued as much for their God-given spiritual gifts as for their ecclesiastical status. It asks us to accept the value of a true lay priesthood, composed of both men and women, joined together as equals in a general assembly of priesthood-holding believers—a reservoir of talent and spiritual power in which the whole church may participate and on which the whole church may rely. It asks us to accept God not merely as one personage, but as two: God the Female and God the Male. In other words, it asks us to accept Christ's female counterpart, the Goddess. For the Bridegroom is not without the Bride. It asks us to accept the view that the feminine is and always has been an integral part of the Christian revelation of the divine nature. And it asks us to accept the equality and mutual interdependence of male and female in the priesthood as a revelation of the very image of that God who is the perfect union of divine male and divine female.

If we can accept the fullness of the godhead in these terms, we are prepared to accept the fullness of the priesthood, which does not refer either to individual or corporate power, but to the power of God bestowed by grace in equal dignity upon males and females alike. I believe we must come to accept the revelation of the fullness of the priesthood to males and females as Joseph Smith's crowning revelation to the church—a revelation given as a comfort and blessing to the Saints in time of travail. Doctrine and Covenants 113 presages such a time, when Zion would find itself in the dust.

Isaiah predicted the time when Zion would be yoked with oppression: "Put on thy strength O Zion!" Joseph Smith's contemporaries asked: "To what people had Isaiah reference to?" Joseph revealed, in response, that Isaiah had reference to those "whom God should call in the last days, who should hold the power of priesthood to bring again Zion, and the redemption of Israel; and to put on her strength is to put on the authority of the priesthood, which Zion has a right to by lineage, and also to return to that power which she had lost" (v. 7-8).

By way of these and other feminine symbols, Joseph Smith called the whole church to accept the doctrine of the fullness of the priesthood of men and women, with all of its implications about the eternality and equality of the sexes. But we have never accepted this teaching. Instead, we find that over 150 years after its founding the church has retreated backward into the comforting dogmas of the early church fathers with all of their prejudices against time, flesh, intuition, and women. I see Mormon feminism as a call to repent— a call to change our minds and come at last to accept time as the mother of eternity, flesh as the sister of the spirit, intuition as the companion of reason, and woman as the equal—the priesthood equal—of man.

I have no way of knowing whether this feminist view will prevail. But I believe that it must attempt to prevail. And I am confident that, should it succeed, Christianity in general and Mormonism in particular will owe to it an incalculable debt which, I believe, will be gratefully acknowledged by both men and women for many generations to come.

The Worship of the Lady

The main contention of Mormon feminism is that God the Mother stands on equal footing with God the Father. There are two primary objections raised against the recogni-

tion and worship of God the Mother as a co-equal member
of the Godhead:

1. Such recognition and worship, especially in the
   form of public or even private prayers to her, consti-
   tutes a contamination of our doctrine, which must be
   kept pure; and

2. There is no precedent in Christianity or Mormonism for worshipping or praying to God the Mother.

I believe both of these objections are substantially without
merit. Let me address, first, the view that worship of God the
Mother is not in keeping with the Mormon view of the
Godhead, which some conservative Mormons contend is
trinitarian. This assertion is so contrary to the doctrine and
history of the church that I hardly know which evidence to
submit first in rebuttal to it. Perhaps it is best to begin with
Joseph Smith's first vision.

Joseph gave several different accounts of this vision, and
from each of them a different God concept can be extracted.
In the earliest recorded version (1832), Joseph reports having
seen only one deity: the Lord Jesus (in Dean C. Jessee, ed.,
Personal Writings of Joseph Smith [Salt Lake City: Deseret Book
Co., 1984], 6). In an 1835 version, he reports having seen two
personages: the Lord and another being—possibly an angel
or the Father (ibid., 75-76). In the 1838 version, eventually
canonized in the Pearl of Great Price, Joseph reports having
seen the Father and the Son (JS-H 2:17). In the *Lectures on
Faith* the Godhead is also portrayed as a duality consisting of
Father and Son (Lec. 5). But in the Doctrine and Covenants
the Godhead is pictured as a trinity: Father, Son, and Holy
Ghost (20:28). The Book of Abraham, on the other hand,

represents the Godhead as a plurality composed of a council of deities, "the Gods" (Abr. 3:22-28; 4). More to the point is a 19 April 1834 vision in which Joseph and others beheld the Father, the Mother, and the Son.

This vision was given while Joseph Smith was travelling from Kirtland to New Portage, Ohio, with Zebedee Coltrin, and either Sidney Rigdon or Oliver Cowdery (or possibly both). Though not reported in the *History of the Church*, 2:50, where mention is made of the New Portage trip, Coltrin gave several accounts of this vision later in his life, one of which was recorded under the date 3 October 1883 in the "Salt Lake School of the Prophets Minutes" (LDS archives):

> Once after returning from a mission, [Coltrin] met Bro. Joseph in Kirtland, who asked him if he did not wish to go with him to a conference at New Portage. The party consisted of Prests. Joseph Smith, Sidney Rigdon, Oliver Cowdry [sic] and myself [Coltrin]. Next morning at New Portage, he [Coltrin] noticed that Joseph seemed to have a far off look in his eyes, or was looking at a distance, and presently he, Joseph, stepped between Brothers Cowdry [sic], and Coltrin and taking them by the arm, said, "lets take a walk." They went to a place where there was beautiful grass, and grapevines and swampbeech interlaced. President Joseph Smith than [sic] said, "Let us pray." They all three prayed in turn—Joseph, Oliver, and Zebedee. Brother Joseph than [sic] said, "now brethren we will see some visions." Joseph lay down on the ground on his back and stretched out his arms and the two brethren lay on them. The heavens gradually opened, and they saw a golden throne, on a circular foundation, something like a lighthouse, and on the throne were

two aged personages, having white hair, and clothed in
white garments. They were the two most beautiful and
perfect specimens of mankind he ever saw. Joseph
said, They are our first parents, Adam and Eve. Adam
was a large broadshouldered man, and Eve a woman,
was large in proportion.

Another version of this vision was recorded by Abraham H.
Cannon in his journal under the date 25 August 1890 (LDS
archives):

Pres. Petersen told of an incident which he often
heard Zebedee Coltrin relate. One day the Prophet
Joseph Smith asked him [Coltrin] and Sidney Rigdon
to accompany him into the woods to pray. When they
had reached a secluded spot Joseph laid down on his
back and stretched out his arms. He told the brethren
to lie one on each arm and then shut their eyes. After
they had prayed he told them to open their eyes. They
did so and they saw a brilliant light surrounding a ped-
estal which seemed to rest on the earth. They closed
their eyes and again prayed. They then saw, on open-
ing them, the Father seated upon a throne; they
prayed again and on looking saw the Mother also; after praying and looking the fourth time they saw the
Savior added to the group. He had auburn brown,
rather long, wavy hair and appeared quite young.

This may be the first recorded vision of the Heavenly Mother
in Mormonism.

In the first of these accounts the Mother is identified as
Eve. In the second she is identified as "The Mother" and is
given status with the Father and the Son. Although this vision

raises theological questions about the nature and number of the Godhead which are beyond the scope of these remarks (see Margaret and Paul Toscano, *Strangers in Paradox* [Salt Lake City: Signature Books, 1990], 60-70), the point is that the Mother is mentioned in conjunction and on an equal footing with the Father and the Son.

Father? Son? Father-Son? Father-Son-Holy Ghost? Father-Mother-Son? A council of Gods? Which is it? Perhaps all. Whatever may be said of Mormons, we are not trinitarians in the ordinary sense. Those who insist that the recognition by Mormons of a Mother in Heaven as a deity co-equal with the Father and the Son does violence to the Mormon doctrine of the trinity—the idea of a cosmic presidency of males—are mistaken since there is no such thing as Mormon trinitarian orthodoxy.

Another point advanced by those opposed to the worship of the Heavenly Mother is that such worship violates our understanding of the proper roles of men and women, with women acting as sustainers and nurturers, men as providers and presiders. The concept of eternal sex roles is raised to support the view that God the Mother cannot be a presiding deity of equal power with the Father and the Son. The rationale behind this view is that, because the sex roles are eternal, Heavenly Mother's eternal role must be that of a nurturer and sustainer. Therefore, she should not be worshipped or prayed to, for these are observances reserved only for those deities who provide and preside—namely, the male deities.

But the scriptures nowhere attest to the propriety of such notions about sex roles. Such ideas are no more scriptural or eternal than the notion that men should be beardless or women should wear bras. These sex roles are cultural conventions borrowed directly from Victorian and post-Victorian society. As Margaret Toscano has argued: "The differences between the sexes, though real and eternal, cannot be translated willy-nilly into sex roles, many of which are stereotypical, artificial, contrived, rigid, and repugnant to the spiritual feelings and experiences of many Church members, male and female alike" (Toscano and Toscano, 279-97). These sex role models contradict the idea set out in Mormon scripture that there is a male and female component in every person, for each of us is "a compound in one" (2 Ne. 2:11)–that is, a composite of two opposing principles, male and female. Therefore, each person is, or at least can be, whole and independent. For this reason, a good marriage does not depend on people living according to these sex roles. Marriage is not meant to make incomplete and codependent individuals whole, but rather to allow whole and independent persons to conjoin into an even greater fullness without obliterating their individuality. In sum, marriage is not the bringing together of two incomplete arcs in an attempt to make a perfect circle. It is the bringing together of perfect equilateral triangles to make a star.

Perhaps the principal reason why sex role models cannot be eternal is because they do not account for the complexity of human sexuality, or for the many instances of role reversals; or for the differences in accepted sex role definitions found among various cultures, or for the psychological and spiritual abuse and damage caused by compelling people, in the name of God, to accept cultural models that do not comport with spiritual reality.

The notion that men should provide and preside while women should nurture and sustain has proven to have been a short-lived domestic formula that is now everywhere being abandoned. Women who have submitted to this concept have not infrequently found themselves deprived of dignity, of material independence, and sometimes even of identity. Many younger couples, often in response to financial necessity, have established their marriages and families on a more equal footing, with man and woman sharing the burdens of providing for and nurturing their families.

In light of both scriptural statements and experiential realities that demonstrate the destructive results of this older view that divides men and women, it is hard to justify the characterization of such roles as divine revelation, rather than as—what they are—the traditions of our fathers and the precepts of men. I agree that recognition of our Mother in Heaven as a member of the Godhead does indeed threaten rigid categories of male and female sex roles. But unlike those who advocate them as God's final word on the relation between the sexes, I welcome this result. Rather than force the Heavenly Mother into an earthly sex role, would it not be less arrogant, and more prudent, to redefine our sex role models to comport with the concept of a Heavenly Mother and a Heavenly Father of equal power and status?

The picture of a submissive and powerless Heavenly Mother is used in Mormonism to reinforce conventional power structures that continue to repress women. For if the Goddess is powerless in heaven, then her daughters must content themselves with that same status on earth. Opponents of the equal status of the Divine Lady find evidence of second-class divinity in the fact that women have not functioned either as authorities of the church or as heavenly messengers—the point being that if women were meant to preside, surely the scriptures would contain some record of it. Thus the claims that females, such as the Virgin Mary, appear from heaven from time to time with messages for a church or for the world are dismissed as ridiculous and false.

They must be false, for they do not fit the current conventional picture of the appropriate female sex role model, and they are not scriptural. It is true that the scriptures are not replete with instances of women presiding or speaking for God or appearing as heraldic angels. But there are notable exceptions to this pattern. In the Book of Mormon, Nephi sees in vision an interpretation of his father Lehi's dream of the Tree of Life. This vision begins with the Virgin Mary, through whom the Messiah is to come. In the Book of Revelation John sees a woman with a crown on her head and twelve stars as bright as the sun with the moon under her feet—symbols which, I believe, indicate that the woman is a sovereign with presiding authority, representing not merely the church, but the Mother Goddess of which the church is a symbol. I should add also that Joseph Smith never denied the validity of the visions claimed by Joan of Arc and St. Teresa, women who claimed visitations from female heraldic angels; rather, Joseph endorsed the visions of these women by having himself sealed to St. Joan and St. Teresa in the new and everlasting covenant of marriage.

Why are such visions of women so rare? Is it because they run contrary to the commandments of God? Or to the precepts of men? God communicates with us mostly in terms we are willing to accept. Perhaps men have not been ready, willing, and able to receive revelations from or about women. But the absence of such things in the past is no reason to believe that such things are not to be. Joseph Smith looked into heaven and said that he could not reveal all he saw. There were things in heaven unlawful to utter on earth. He said he only told a hundredth part of what he could have revealed (Joseph Fielding Smith, comp., *Teachings of the Prophet Joseph Smith* [Salt Lake City: Deseret Book Co., 1964], 304-305). He said that if a person looked into heaven for five minutes that person would know more about it than has ever been written about the subject (ibid., 324). If the scriptures are silent or deficient on a point, we cannot conclude the negative proposition with respect to that point. Scriptural silence does not mean that no female angels make visitations, that women should be denied priesthood, or that Heavenly Mother should not be acknowledged, worshipped, or invoked in prayer.

The tendency to treat scriptural silence as a prohibition led to the rejection of Jesus as Messiah. The Old Testament, while stressing the concept of one true God, is silent on the divinity of the Messiah or his identity as God's son. This lack of information was construed by many as a negative statement: Because the Torah said there was only one God, the claim that Jesus was God's son and Messiah was rejected as blasphemous.

In like manner, the scriptures seem to say little or nothing about the restoration of the gospel, the flesh-and-bone body of God, the need for prophets and apostles and continuing revelation, the coming forth of the Book of Mormon, etc. Yet after these things became part of received Mormon tradition, the scriptures were consulted again and found to contain evidence, not conclusive but indicative, to support all these points.

The same will be true of the doctrine of the Heavenly Mother. When we come to accept the Heavenly Mother, we will discover that she has not been grafted into the Godhead at the last moment to satisfy the desires of feminists, but that she was in fact an active and co-equal member of the Godhead all along—and we will find scriptural evidence to support this. We will eventually see that her nurturing and chastising spirit was always part of the Judeo-Christian tradition as the *Hokmah* and the *Shekinah* of Hebrew tradition. We will make arguments that the Holy Spirit, with its rebirthing, nurturing, rebuking, comforting, blessing, healing, and maturing functions, its constant companionship, its constant testifying of Jesus Christ, its ever-presence with us on the earth calling us to full spirituality, appears to meet the expectations of a caring, divine mother ever present among her children.

Another argument against the equality of the Woman of Holiness is that women are prohibited from receiving instructions for the church. This prohibition is not found in scripture, but in tradition. In fact, scripture contradicts this tradition. According to Doctrine and Covenants 25, Emma Smith and all other women of the church are to be "ordained" (v. 7) to "expound scripture and to exhort the Church, according as it shall be given . . . by my Spirit." The point of these verses is that women should not be concerned merely with the menial or the domestic (v. 10), but the spiritual and the eternal. They are to be ordained to expound and exhort. If women are not to receive instruction for the church, then how can they keep God's commandment "to exhort the Church, according as it shall be given . . . by my Spirit"?

In keeping with Doctrine and Covenants 25, Wilford Woodruff, while president of the church, declared in 1892 not only the right but the necessity for women of the church to receive revelation:

Oh! Ye Latter-day Saints, you talk about revelation, and wonder if there is any revelation. Why, bless your souls, say nothing about the apostles and elders around me, these mountains contain thousands upon thousands of devoted women, holy women, righteous women, virtuous women, who are filled with the inspiration of Almighty God. . . . Yes, we have revelation. The Church of God could not live twenty-four hours without revelation (G. Homer Durham, ed., *The Discourses of Wilford Woodruff* [Salt Lake City: Bookcraft, 1969], 61-62).

The Old Testament tells us that God calls on women. Think of the work of God done through Rahab (Josh. 2), or of the rights and blessings of the priesthood transmitted to Isaac, not through Abraham alone, but through Sarah as well (Gen. 17-18), of the prophetic callings of Miriam (Ex. 15:20), Noadiah (Neh. 6:14), Deborah (Judg. 4-5), and Huldah (2 Kgs. 22:14; 2 Chr. 34:22).

In the New Testament we are told that women prayed and prophesied in the Christian church (1 Cor. 11:15), practices that were forbidden to women in Jewish congregations. Also we have evidence that women performed missionary work and functioned as leaders of Christian households. The four daughters of Philip the Seventy were acknowledged to be prophetesses (Acts 21:9). Paul commends the women Priscilla, Mary, Tryphena, and Tryphosa for their important work. In Romans 16:1-2 the woman Phoebe is identified as a deacon of the church. And in Romans 16:7 Paul accounts Junia, a female, as one of note among the apostles.

It is not likely that these are textual corruptions, but rather remnants of references to the priesthood in the primitive church, references that had not been sanitized from the texts by later editors looking to harmonize the scriptures with the developing view of women as inferior—a view advanced not by the early apostles, but by later Christians under the influence of ancient Greek philosophy and misogyny.

In addition to this evidence there is the testimony of

the Gospels that the first witnesses of the resurrection and its angelic heralds were the women who had known Jesus during his life and ministry. Mary Magdalene was the first to see and touch him. Women were first to bear this special witness to the incredulous male apostles and disciples. Since that day, women have been engaged in the ministry, writing hymns, preaching, expounding, and exhorting. Clearly, God has and does work through women. The fact that so many women are feeling the need to recognize and worship our Mother in Heaven is, perhaps, another instance of God working through women to bless the Saints with revelations and to move the church toward greater spiritual maturity.

In my view the most profound problem with opponents of the Goddess is that they manifest a fundamentally flawed understanding of the gospel and mission of Jesus Christ. Before Christ, holiness was defined in Judaism mostly in terms of strict compartmentalization, of separation from the unholy and the unclean. Jews were to separate themselves from gentiles and heathen. Milk and meat were not to be mixed. Ritual cleansings were required if the Law of Moses was violated. Priesthood was bestowed only on males of certain lineages. Holiness and cleanliness before God were seen in terms of strict obedience to law and tradition. Women were seen as inferior to men—so inferior they were considered a reproach.

Jesus swept all this away. A new covenant was established. This was the good news—the gospel. In Christ, gentiles were placed on an equal footing with Jews, black on an equal footing with white, slave on an equal footing with free, and female on an equal footing with male (Gal. 3:28). Salvation was made free and available to all who would partake. It was milk and honey without price. The priesthood too was vouch-safed to men and women alike, for it was revealed as a priesthood without father, without mother, without descent, without beginning of days or end of life (Heb. 7:3). Faith in Christ, not lineage or gender, became the only condition for priesthood ordination.

In keeping with the revelation of the gospel through Jesus Christ, Joseph Smith promised the restored priesthood in its fullness to women (Andrew Ehat and Lyndon Cook, eds., *The Words of Joseph Smith* [Provo, UT: BYU Religious Studies Center, 1980], 119). This promise suggests that men and women are to be equal. Equality is the jewel in the crown of Mormon scripture and theology: God in the person of Christ Jesus was made equal to us so that we might be made equal to him. We are to be equal in earthly things and in heavenly things (D&C 78:6). Women and men are to be equal in the Lord. They are to be equal in spiritual gifts and priestly rights. Like Abraham and Sarah, they are to be priests and priestesses, kings and queens, with the promise of holding the powers of heaven jointly.

Doctrine and Covenants 132 contains a revelation about the status of men and women in the new and everlasting covenant of marriage. There are problems in the tone of certain portions of this text. Perhaps some of Joseph's anger and frustration with his wife Emma (much of which cannot be justified from our perspective) seeps in. But the theological core of this revelation stands apart from the marital discord of the Smiths. This core theology does not put the man ahead of the woman. It does not marginalize the woman. The man and the woman are spoken of here as equals. The central verses of this revelation state that when a man and woman are married and sealed in the new and everlasting covenant and all power is committed to them by the oath and covenant of God, their names are written in the Lamb's book of life. They become gods. They have no end and are from everlasting to everlasting (vv. 19-20).

The doctrine of equality in spiritual powers and gifts was further advanced by Joseph Smith when he taught that the fullness of the priesthood is to be conferred on the man and woman jointly (*Teachings of the Prophet Joseph Smith*, 321), and that through faith and the voluntary acceptance of the ordinances the man and woman would become joint heirs of Jesus Christ. This is the pattern of deification. To this point, Apostle Erastus Snow addressed himself on March 3, 1878:

> If I believe anything that God has ever said about himself, and anything pertaining to the creation and organization of man upon the earth, I must believe that Deity consists of man and woman . . . there can be no God except he is composed of the man and woman united, and there is not in all the eternities that exist, nor ever will be, a God in any other way . . . . There never was a God, and there never will be in all the eternities, except they are made of these two component parts: a man and a woman; the male and the female (*Journal of Discourses* 19:269-70).

Even as conservative a Mormon theologian as Bruce R. McConkie has written that "an exalted and glorified Man of Holiness . . . could not be a Father unless a Woman of like glory, perfection, and holiness was associated with him as a Mother" (*Mormon Doctrine* [Salt Lake City: Bookcraft, 1966], 516).

This evidence points to the conclusion that our Mother in Heaven is the equal of our Father in Heaven—a woman of equal stature, who holds with him jointly and equally the powers of heaven. This tells us that the Mother in Heaven is a genuine deity, a Goddess, equal in her godhood with the other members of the Godhead. If there is a dearth of information about this being, it is due, I think, to plain and precious things being taken from the scriptures and to our hard-heartedness in refusing to accept the implications of this revelation. The point is that if the church forbids the worship and prayerful invocation of God the Mother as a presiding member of the Christian Godhead, then the church is in fact rejecting the equality of women and men in general and the equality of the Woman of Holiness, the Man of Holiness, and the Son of Righteousness in particular. Are we truly prepared, now, on the record before us, to make such a rejection?

With respect to the specific issue of praying to the Heavenly Mother, let me observe that Mormons have been praying to her for years. Doctrine and Covenants 25:12 tells us that the song of the righteous is a prayer that will be answered with blessings upon our heads. Since October 1845 the Saints have been singing and praying to their Mother and Father in heaven in the following words of Eliza R. Snow's hymn:

> When I leave this frail existence,
> When I lay this mortal by,
> Father, Mother, may I meet you
> In your royal courts on high?
> Then at length when I've completed
> All you sent me forth to do,
> With your mutual approbation
> May I come and dwell with you?

If this is not a prayer, then there never has been a prayer

uttered in Christendom. It is a prayer not just to the Father, but to the Father and the Mother:

Father, Mother, may I meet you in your royal courts on high?

Linda Wilcox provides evidence that both the concept of the Heavenly Mother and the prayer to the Father and the Mother were revealed to Eliza R. Snow by Joseph Smith: Although President Wilford Woodruff gave Eliza R. Snow credit for originating the idea—"That hymn is a revelation, though it was given to us by a woman"—it is more likely that Joseph Smith was the first to expound the doctrine of a Mother in Heaven. Joseph F. Smith claimed that "God revealed that principle that we have a mother as well as a father in heaven to Joseph Smith; Joseph Smith revealed it to Eliza Snow Smith, his wife; and Eliza Snow was inspired, being a poet, to put it into verse" (in Maureen Ursenbach Beecher and Lavina Fielding Anderson, eds., *Sisters in Spirit* [Urbana: University of Illinois Press, 1987], 66).

Wilcox also states that Susa Young Gates claimed the doctrine of a Mother in Heaven came from Joseph Smith. Gates further reported that Joseph Smith told Zina D. Huntington, on the death of Zina's mother in 1839, that Zina would not only meet her earthly mother, but would also "meet and become acquainted with [the] Eternal Mother, the wife of your Father in Heaven" (ibid., 66). Wilcox notes that a number of sources suggest that Eliza R. Snow and Brigham Young believed Eve to be the Mother in Heaven (ibid.).

The Woman of Holiness has been and is being worshipped by Mormons. Many have come to understand that she is not just a heavenly housewife or a domesticated divinity who stands quietly and patiently three steps behind her husband and son, but that she is an equal in the Godhead. There is nothing in the scriptures or teachings of the prophets to suggest that she is inferior. There is evidence to the contrary.

Is it wise then in light of these teachings and practices to relegate the Mother of Life to the status of a second-rate deity—or, worse, to treat her as if she were a fiction—or to forbid her worship as idolatry, especially in light of the revered place she holds in Mormon theology and of the powerful spiritual experiences that many people have had and are having with her—experiences that have fortified their faith in Christ? The Book of Mormon encourages us to follow after those things that lead us to Christ. Does recognition of a heavenly mother detract from the centrality of the Son any more than the recognition of a heavenly father?

Worship, real worship, cannot be dictated. Worship is to move from grace to grace. It is contact with the divine. It is to grow in the knowledge of the mystery that is God. People cannot just shunt aside their spiritual experiences as if they did not exist. Nor should they be forbidden from approaching God by whatever paths God reveals. The Mother has been revealed to Mormons. The revelation cannot now be unspoken, even if it is yet to be fully accepted and appreciated.

It is my hope that we will be neither fearful nor narrow-minded, and that as a church and a people we will neither forbid nor discourage either the worship or prayerful invocation of God the Mother, said in the name of Jesus Christ, nor the recognition of the Holy Mother as part of the Christian Godhead. To those who would forbid such, let me paraphrase the warning given by Gamaliel to the Sanhedrin, inclined to forbid the worship of Jesus Christ: You men of Israel! Take heed to yourselves as to what you intend to do with these people. Refrain from troubling them. Let them alone. For if this work be of human origin, then it will come to nothing. But if it be of divine origin, you cannot overthrow it and what is worse you may in your ignorant zeal inadvertently find yourselves fighting against God (Acts 5:34-35, 38-39).

Chapter Six.

SILVER AND GOLD HAVE I NONE

"Silver and Gold Have I None" was originally a presentation given at the Sunstone Theological Symposium in August 1991 as part of a panel given in response to a series of articles on church finances published in the Arizona Republic.

Recently the *Arizona Republic* ran a series of investigative reports on the LDS church's financial holdings and operations. As I read them, an uneasiness grew inside me. At first I did not know why.

The articles made it clear that no scandals, illegalities, or improprieties in the management of the church's finances had been uncovered. And they confirmed to me what I had already suspected: the church takes in a great deal of money; its asset base is large; its investments are prudently made and managed; and, because the church's policy is to avoid debt, the majority of its assets are free and clear of encumbrances. There is nothing in any of this to cause alarm. If anything, this information should have been to me what it was to many Latter-day Saints—a source of gratitude and even pride.

That the church should have a temporal dimension has never troubled me. One contribution that Mormonism makes to Christianity is the revelation of the balance of physical and spiritual. Where traditional Christianity has long viewed the physical world as weakening and disabling, Joseph Smith's teachings link embodiment with spiritual empowerment. Embodiment manifests itself in various ways, including the legal and economic arrangements by which a society maintains itself and prospers. These societal structures comprise the body politic, the body of the community. In Mormonism the temporal stands on an equal footing with the spiritual. Both are equally important in the development and sanctification of individuals and of communities. For this reason, we Mormons have always believed that wealth can be a great blessing.

In spite of my acceptance of these ideas, the uneasiness I felt about the *Arizona Republic* articles persisted for two reasons: First, Mormonism's gentle view of materiality was never meant to serve as a justification for economic non-disclosure. Nevertheless, non-disclosure is one of the pillars of the church's financial management policy. This policy can be stated as a paraphrase of the 9th Article of Faith: When it comes to matters of money, the church has revealed very little, it does now reveal very little, and it will yet refuse to reveal many great and important things pertaining to the economics of the kingdom of God.

The news articles are noteworthy precisely because they confound this policy by presenting information about the church's finances that is so difficult to acquire. But why? Why as members of the church aren't we informed about these things by our leaders? Why must we always learn these things, harmless as they are, in the streets?

The usual response is that the payment of tithing is an act of faith. The earth is the Lord's and the fullness thereof. To pay tithing is to render to God what is God's. His servants, the church leaders, hold the tithing funds and all other church property in trust—not for the Saints—but for the Lord. Once we pay our donations, the money is out of our hands. We have no right to inquire into its disposition. It falls within the exclusive province of the Brethren. Those of us who are inclined to raise questions about the management of the church's wealth are said to be in spiritual jeopardy, for our questioning will inevitably lead to sadness, inactivity, transgression, and apostasy.

I accept that the wealth of the church, like the Sabbath day, is consecrated to God. But I also believe that, like the Sabbath, this wealth was meant for our benefit. Church members are the beneficiaries of the trust between God (the trustor) and the leaders of the church (the trustees). As such, church members have certain rights and entitlements that are expressed or implied in various scriptural narratives.

The Old Testament story of Samuel and Saul suggests that God disfavors closed hierarchical rule as typified by a monarchy and favors instead more open participatory government as typified by the system of judges. This preference is reinforced in the New Testament where both leaders and members are depicted as participating in the most sacred and most important business of the church: the calling of the apostle Matthias to replace Judas Iscariot and the resolution by the council of Jerusalem of the "gentile question." The Doctrine and Covenants explicitly states that "all things [are to] be done in order and by common consent in the Church" (22:13) and that church leaders are forbidden to exercise unrighteous dominion, including, certainly, the suppression of information, which is, in the modern world, one of the chief ways to maintain control. Jesus commands open disclosure when he requires his followers neither to cover their sins nor to hide their light under a bushel.

These narratives and revelations imply a divine preference for open and participatory church governance on the basis of the informed common consent of the members. This makes sense. If, as section 105, states, the Saints must grow in knowledge and in experience, then, for the sake of our spiritual growth, we must be informed of its temporal and spiritual affairs and be included at some meaningful level in its governance. Less than this is to reduce the governance of the church from a democratic theocracy to an oligarchy.

In addition to these scriptural statements, there are certain legal requirements that come into play. Is not the church a non-profit corporation sole? Are not the leaders of the church its trustees? Do they not, therefore, have a fiduciary duty to make regular detailed public accountings of the trust? In a recent general priesthood meeting President Gordon B. Hinckley admitted that such an accounting was owed. But a proper accounting has yet to be made. The failure to make this accounting is usually excused on grounds that church business is private business. But is the church a private organization? Are the scriptures, the doctrines, the blessings of the gospel, and the spiritual mission of the church private property? Is the kingdom of God the private possession of any man or group of men? Do we not all share an interest in it? And though we may not all have an equal say in its management, is there any good reason why a proper public accounting cannot regularly be provided? Would not such an accounting tend to assure circumspection in our dealings and remove any suggestion of impropriety or self-dealing?

Of course, in response to all this we are likely to be told that if we believe our leaders are called of God then why don't we trust them with the church's wealth? This question, however, can be turned around: If we are the people of God, why can't we be trusted with an accounting? Trust, I suspect, is not the real issue here. The issue is control. Church leaders are like many of our parents and their generation who believe that their children should know little or nothing about the family's finances. The problem with this view is that our leaders are not our parents. We have heavenly parents. Our leaders are our elder siblings, who, it seems, are tempted to generate policies that tend to lull many of their more compliant brothers and sisters into complacency, inexperience, and unhealthy dependency.

Another reason why these articles make me uneasy is because of the extent of the church's wealth. Though this may have been overstated in the articles, the truth is that the church is rich. Why must the church have so much money? Especially since it has been acquired by the sacrifice of so many of its members. I believe in sacrifice. Our religion is founded upon a sacrifice. Jesus asks us to imitate him and to bear one another's burden's that they may be light. This is the point of the parable of the good Samaritan. What troubles me is that, in spite of its affluence, the institutional church seems unwilling to sacrifice or to bear the burdens of others.

One of the most grievous burdens which Latter-day Saints are required to bear is caused by the tithing system, which is so sacrosanct that rarely do we read or hear any discussions or evaluations of it. Doctrine and Covenants 119 contains the revelation which serves as the source of the requirement that members pay to the church one tenth of all our "interest" or "surplus." "Interest" refers to money or property in excess of principal. "Surplus" refers to what is left over after necessary expenses are paid. A tithe on interest or surplus is fair because necessaries are first paid for, then the surplus becomes the basis on which the tithing is calculated. The greater one's surplus the greater her or his tithe.

But the church general handbook, the guidebook for church administrators, states that "interest" and "surplus" are interpreted by modern church leaders to mean income. Income refers either to gross income, which is the value of all money or property earned within a given period, without deductions of any kind, or to net income (also called disposable income), which is the value of all money or property earned after taxes are deducted. A tithe based on income, gross or net, is regressive; in other words, it is more burdensome for the poor than the rich. The rich can pay a tithe on a substantial income out of discretionary funds and continue to afford both necessaries and luxuries. The poor, in many instances, can pay tithing on income only if they sacrifice not mere luxuries, but necessities.

I don't mean to suggest that those who pay tithing at a sacrifice are not blessed or that sacrifice is not required of us by God. I mean only to point out that because we are required to tithe our income instead of our interest or surplus, our tithing requirement systematically disfavors the poor and favors the rich. This system is even less acceptable in light of the information contained in the *Arizona Republic*. For it is clear that many faithful Saints are scrimping and sacrificing to pay tithing to assist not a poor, floundering, economically troubled church, but a very rich church. Many Mormons sustain multiple employment and many leave young children at home to supplement their earnings so that they can continue to pay a full tithing on income in order to hold temple recommends and to remain qualified for church administrative callings. Other members borrow to pay their tithing, thus becoming debtors so that the church may continue to avoid debt. They mortgage their property so that the church may hold its properties without mortgages. Can it be the will of a God, who freely sacrificed his eternal life, that the church that bears his name, while flush with wealth, continues to deflect its liabilities to the Saints, many of whom cannot readily bear such a burden? Doesn't this amount to the activity condemned by Jesus, the sin of binding heavy burdens and grievous to be borne and laying them on people's shoulders and refusing to lift them?

The Lord taught us to pray "forgive us our debts as we forgive our debtors." But how can the church utter this prayer? It has no debts. Perhaps for this reason it finds it difficult to forgive the debts of others. Jesus said "love one another as I have loved you," and then he himself carried on his accounts the entire debt of mortal sin and imperfection. But the church does not seem willing to put up with sin, imperfection, or debt.

Jesus said, you cannot be equal in heavenly things until you are first equal in earthly things. But in the church are we equal in earthly things? Are we equal in the knowledge of the church's accumulated wealth?

The church, it seems, wants our obedience not our desires. It wants our compliance, not our concerns. It wants us to line up, quietly, on the asset side of its ledgers. Those who oppose it, even in loyal opposition, become liabilities and are, publicly or privately, written off its books.

In one dire prophesy of the Book of Mormon we read: "Your churches, yea every one, have become polluted because of the pride of your hearts. For behold, ye do love money and your substance and your fine apparel and the adorning of your churches, more than ye love the poor and the needy, and the sick and the afflicted. O ye pollutions, ye hypocrites, ye teachers, who sell yourselves for that which will canker, why have ye polluted the holy church of God?" (Morm. 8:36-37) Why is it so difficult for us to remember not to trust in the arm of flesh, not to lay up for ourselves treasures upon earth, where moth and rust corrupt and thieves break through and steal?

There are reasons. And I would be unfair and uncompromising in my criticisms not to mention them. I think the chief reason why the church manages its finances without disclosure, without participation, without liberality, is fear. This reason should not be underestimated: The church has been persecuted. It was driven from its property. Its property was escheated. It was disincorporated. It was once deeply in debt. To this day it continues to be shamed and ridiculed, not for its sins, but for its spirituality, for its beliefs, for its allegiance to sacral but politically incorrect teachings. Fear is a powerful motive. Perhaps as a church we see wealth as a means to insulate us from pain, to make sure that the persecutions and rejections of the past will not deeply wound us again. This is understandable. It explains in part our secretive ways, our need for power, wealth, and a good public image. But this has not given rise to wise policy.

The tragic flaw in Shakespeare's *Timon of Athens* was that Timon was never able to shake his obsession with wealth, his addiction to gold, "yellow, glittering, precious gold," which

> . . . will make black white, foul fair,
> Wrong right, base noble, old young, coward valiant. . . .
> This yellow slave
> Will knit and break religions, bless the accursed,
> Make the hoar leprosy adored, place thieves,
> And give them title, knee, and approbation
> With senators on the bench. This is it
> That makes the wappened widow wed again—
> . . . —this embalms and spices
> To the April day again (*Timon of Athens*, IV, iii, 26-41).

"This yellow slave will knit and break religions . . ." The question is, will gold knit or break Mormonism? I do not know. But I do not believe that Zion will be redeemed by gold. Zion will be redeemed, like we are redeemed, by blood—the blood of Jesus Christ, which blood is the token of his unconditional love for us. Moroni's warning was, I think, not just to Joseph Smith but to the whole church he was yet to establish: the treasure is not gold, but the word of God that is written in gold. We seem not to have understood this warning. The church and its best and brightest are not immune from the lust to have more and more and from the fear of poverty and powerlessness. The apostles of old worried that there would not be enough—only a few fishes and a few loaves for so many—but when the multitude had been fed, there were twelve baskets of bread and twelve baskets of fish, enough for the twelve, and the seventy, and to spare. Later they came to accept that Christ's kingdom is not of this world, that the riches of the kingdom are the mysteries of God, that the treasures of the church are its faithful adherents. Somehow we must resist the temptation to administer the church by calculation, rather than compassion, by fear rather than love. If we seek the love of God and impart it to others, we will be able to freely give as we have freely received, to feed the hungry, clothe the naked, heal the sick, comfort the wretched, give to the needy—and all without worrying if there will be enough. The truth is there isn't enough of anything but love. It is only through love that we can resist the temptation to put our trust in silver and gold and the safety net of net worth.

I say all this shamefaced. For I must confess that I find it much easier to believe in money than in miracles and to retreat into selfishness rather than to make myself vulnerable for the sake of others. I have never found it easy to make money, but I have found it much easier than to say, "Silver and gold have I none; but such as I have give I thee: In the name of Jesus Christ of Nazareth rise up and walk," and with those words to heal the lame, the halt, the blind, the feeble, the sick, and the broken-hearted. But though we are all imperfect, should we not as a church and a people distinguish ourselves from other earthly institutions by relying less on riches and more on the grace and spirit of Christ Jesus?

I will close with a tale that sums up my point: In the sixth century Benedict of Nursia, the father of Western monasticism, was censured by the Catholic church for his heretical views on the holiness of poverty. In due course he was summoned before the Pope. Though in fear for his life Benedict obeyed. The Pope was gracious and, to put the monk at ease, showed him the treasures of the church. When the tour was over, the Pope announced, "Peter can no longer say, Silver and gold have I none." "Yes," replied Benedict sadly, "but neither can he say, arise and walk."

Chapter Seven.

DEALING WITH
SPIRITUAL ABUSE

*"Dealing with Spiritual Abuse" was originally a presentation
given at the Sunstone Theological Symposium in August 1992.*

I have not borne my testimony on fast Sunday in church for
well over a decade. I don't know why: reticence, frustration,
disappointment, small children underfoot, perhaps grief or
a rapid succession of painful paradigm shifts. But at the
outset I have decided to make a public statement of my
religious beliefs because it may help clarify why I have concluded that an organization like the Mormon Alliance is
urgently needed in the Mormon community. (The Mormon
Alliance was organized in 1992 as a non-profit corporation
to counter defamation of and spiritual abuse in the church.)
   I believe that I exist, that you exist, and that we inhabit
a cosmos ordered upon principles that are complex, obscure,
maddeningly elusive, and in a state of flux. I believe the
natural world I experience with my senses is real, but that its
exact nature lies beyond human sensory capacity, even when
enhanced by technology. I believe we humans and our un-
derstandings are limited and imperfect. I believe that, for the

109

foreseeable future, we must content ourselves with perceptions of truth rather than with truth itself.

Because I believe we exist, it is easy for me to believe that God exists. Our existence makes probable the existence of other intelligent beings. If there is one intelligent being, and another more intelligent, there is probably another more intelligent than the first two. The most intelligent of all these is God. This is not proof, I know. For this reason I sometimes doubt the reality of the spiritual world and life after death. I am a child of my generation. I have existential angst. My doubts, though, are mostly emotional. At bottom I believe in life after death because I have experienced life before death. To me eternal life seems no more amazing than mortal life; and the reality of immortal souls, no more implausible than the reality of mortal bodies.

I believe in an other-dimensional, spiritual realm that is co-extensive with the natural. The two are intertwined and interdependent. The natural world gives shape to the spiritual, while the spiritual gives life to the natural. They relate to each other like blood to the body, like oxygen to the blood. I believe this not because I have seen into the spiritual world with my natural eyes, but because I have seen into myself. The kingdom of God is within each of us. Our access to the spiritual world is primarily through our own being. The way to the spirit world is not upward, but inward. Of course, there is no proof of this either. Proof is natural and outward. I believe in proof, when I can get it. But I also believe in experience. We experience the spiritual world when we think, or calculate, or discern, when we respond to beauty or truth, when we suffer or doubt, when we love or hate, when we dream, and even when we despair. I despair sometimes because I cannot know the spiritual world as I know the natural, but neither can I know that natural world as I do the spiritual. The natural world seems to me so real and yet so meaningless, while the supernatural world seems so unreal and yet so full of significance.

I believe the most significant element of the spiritual world is God; and I believe the most significant aspect of God is that God did not choose to be insulated from the natural world. This is why I am a Christian: I believe that God entered the world with all its pain and limitations in the person of Jesus of Nazareth. He is Lord and Savior. He atoned for our sins and loves us in our sins and imperfections and was willing to make himself less than we are so that we could be made equal to God. I accept without reservation the gospel of Jesus Christ. I am not ashamed of it. I believe also in the existence of a goddess, a female counterpart to Christ, a Bride of the Bridegroom. She is his equal. She too descended to earth to be our constant companion, to mourn with us, comfort us, reprove us, inspire us, bring us into a newness of life, and lead us into all truth. This Lord and Lady are equal partners in our creation, redemption, and exaltation. The purpose of existence is to know them as we are known by them and to share with them eternal life. With divine help mortals are capable of becoming like them. I believe this because we have longings to be good and fair and just and merciful, even if we cannot perfectly achieve these things. Some people have made the journey to spiritual maturation and have entered into the presence of God. I believe in angels and devils, in spirits good and bad. I believe some angelic beings visit the earth and live among us as mortals to share our pains and griefs. I believe heraldic angels sometimes visit mortals with personal messages and with messages for others. Some people are born with the gift to perceive the supernatural world.

I believe Joseph Smith was one of these people—a man gifted and flawed, spiritual and natural, careless and caring, passionate and aloof, known for good and evil. I believe he saw angels who conferred on him spiritual power and authority by which he revealed the mind and will of God through scriptural texts. Taken together, these texts proclaim the gospel of Jesus Christ with clarity and set forth a cosmogony, cosmology, angiology, soteriology, and eschatology that is as rich as it is undervalued.

I believe people are called of God to their spiritual convictions. Some are called to one religion, some to another, and some to none at all. Some have the gift to believe; others have the gift to be skeptics. Some are called by birth; others, by rebirth. All are precious in the sight of God. Each is deserving of the understanding and respect of the others. For those called by birth or rebirth to be Latter-day Saints, the Church of Jesus Christ of Latter-day Saints is the only true and living church on the face of the whole earth. This is not to deny the truths to which God has called others, nor to assert that the LDS church is above criticism, it is only to reaffirm the truths to which God has called us Mormons.

I believe in the restoration of the priesthood and of the church and in the gift of apostles, prophets, pastors, evangelists, and teachers. I believe that the church is good and is capable of greater good, and that God has called Latter-day Saints, leaders and members, to repent and forgive, to be vulnerable to pain and reproach without responding in kind, and to bring good out of evil. I believe in the spiritual efficacy of the ordinances of the gospel, the endowment, the sealings, the new and everlasting covenant of marriage, and in vicarious ordinances for the dead.

I believe in the fruits and gifts of the spirit and that all these blessings have been given to the Latter-day Saints to help us build Zion—a true community that eschews selfishness, lust, greed, elitism, self-righteousness, xenophobia, sexism, homophobia, and authoritarianism and is founded upon the principles of justice, fairness, mercy, equality, truth, and charity—the mutual, reciprocal, and unconditional love of God. I believe in the institutions of church and state and that they should (1) guarantee to all individuals the right to develop their gifts, characteristics, talents, dignity, personhood, and potentials, (2) restrict the arbitrary use of power upon any individuals or institutions, and (3) encourage the growth and development of voluntary communities based upon free and open covenants. In the words of my friend Fred Voros, I believe that baptism washes away our sins, not our rights. I believe it is consistent with my faith as a Christian and a Mormon to write and speak my views, to disagree even with my leaders, and to state my dissent and my reasons therefor and, if I am ignored, to raise my voice, to express my distress or indignation, and even to resort to sarcasm and satire. I believe in this because I love Mormonism and want to see it flourish. I have made this statement because I wish to show that I have worked to resist spiritual abuse and to assist its victims not as an outsider, but as a believing Mormon.

Cardinal among my beliefs is that unrighteous dominion, spiritual abuse, theological correctness, and ecclesiastical tyranny are utterly repugnant to the teachings of Jesus Christ, to the assumptions and aspirations of the restoration, and to the goals and objectives of the LDS church. In saying this I do not indulge a juvenile idealism that lusts for human perfection. I am not talking about personal human foibles. I have already said that I believe in human limitations and imperfections and in the need to repent and forgive. I condemn not people but bad principles, not our heritage but false traditions, not our leaders but unwholesome teachings, damaging expectations, and unjust procedures that tend to create a climate of intimidation and to justify spiritual abuse.

I have used the term "spiritual abuse" both in the title and text of these remarks. I learned that term from a book entitled *The Subtle Power of Spiritual Abuse*, by David Johnson and Jeff VanVonderen. The authors are Christian ministers. Their book is not about Mormonism, but about spiritual abuse in Protestantism. Without intending to do so, these authors describe with disturbing accuracy many abusive practices of the LDS church. The authors, unfortunately, do not provide a reliable, formal definition of spiritual abuse. However, Margaret Toscano, Fred Voros, and James Gardner (my nephew) have helped to create such a definition.

The short version is this: Spiritual abuse is the persistent exercise of power by spiritual or ecclesiastical leaders in a way that serves the demands of the leaders to the detriment of the members. The long version is more complex, but necessary if spiritual abuse is to be distinguished from mere insults, violence, or other forms of hurt. Spiritual abuse is the persistent exploitation by spiritual or ecclesiastical leaders in a religious system of an imbalance of power between the leaders and the followers, whereby the leaders maintain control through the exercise of their authority without adequate accountability by taking actions, making definitions, creating rules, or rendering judgments that are unfair, unequal, and nonreciprocal, while taking advantage of or promoting the inexperience, ignorance, fear, confusion, weakness, or delusion of the followers, in order to perpetuate the power imbalance and thereby gratify temporarily the demands of the leaders or the perceived interests of the ecclesiastical institution to the detriment and at the expense of the spiritual needs, rights, entitlements, dignities, or empowerment of the followers. Let me illustrate these generalities with some specifics.

Legalism, or performance preoccupation. The most spiritually abusive behavior or attitude identified by Johnson and VanVonderen is legalism, or performance preoccupation. Legalism is a form of religious perfectionism that focuses on the careful performance of some behaviors and the careful avoidance of others. Religiously legalistic people feel that spirituality is the payment we receive for doing good works, rather than a gift from God which empowers us to do good works. The problem with legalism is that (a) it emphasizes material or visible success and outward respectability rather than holiness, (b) it values image over individual or community spirituality, (c) it leads people to view God not as a loving Savior, but as a relentless taskmaster, never satisfied, vindictive, distant, and intolerant of even the slightest mistake, (d) it promotes the judgment of others' performance rather than personal repentance, and (e) it can cause leaders to promote statistically verifiable works to justify continued use of compulsory means.

Power posturing. Johnson and VanVonderen write: "Power-posturing simply means that leaders spend a lot of time focused on their own authority and reminding others of it, as well. This is necessary because their spiritual authority isn't real—based on genuine godly character—it is postured" (63-64). This is an obvious problem in the LDS church, where the watch-cry is no longer "Holiness to the Lord," but "Follow the Brethren." The over-emphasis on obedience to church leaders, if continued unabated, will eclipse personal revelation, personal responsibility, and personal devotion, and will eventually end in a leadership that is out of touch with reality or corrupted by special privilege.

Shaming. Shaming is another spiritually abusive technique. It includes name calling, belittling, put downs, comparing the abused unfavorably with others, and wrongful and unjustified discipline. The most memorable example of this technique I can recall occurred when Apostle Bruce R. McConkie went to Brigham Young University and, in an address delivered to 12,000 or so students and faculty, publicly denounced certain passages of George Pace's book on developing a personal relationship with Christ. Elder McConkie gave no prior warning of his intentions, made no prior attempt to work things out privately with Brother Pace, engaged in no prior discussions to understand Brother Pace's message. Elder McConkie merely shamed Brother Pace before his peers and students, not by name, but in such a way that there could be no doubt who was meant. Although I have been told by more than one insider that Brother McConkie later expressed regret for this incident, he never apologized publicly; and George Pace has born the scars of this humiliation for years. This is an act of spiritual abuse, but no more so than shaming people by calling them apostates, anti-Mormon, or enemies of the church, when there is neither basis in fact nor justifiable reason to do so.

Secretiveness: Johnson and VanVonderen say, "When you see people in a religious system being secretive—*watch out.* People don't hide what is appropriate; they hide what is inappropriate" (78). This is not to gainsay the need for confidentiality with respect to personal finances, health, family issues, and victimless transgressions, so long as the confidentiality is intended to protect the member. In Mormonism, however, secretiveness, especially with respect to such community issues as our history, our finances, and the deliberations of the church's governing councils is legendary. Church leaders wrongly justify secretiveness for public relations reasons—to protect the good name or image of the church; or leaders, expressing a patronizing view, insist that members be treated like children and given "milk before meat," even if they are sick to death of milk and are dying for meat and potatoes. *The demand for "Peace and Unity."* True peace and unity are important spiritual values. But, to quote Johnson and VanVonderen: "experiencing true peace and unity does not mean pretending to get along or acting like we agree when we don't" (90). Pseudo-community is a term used by Scott Peck in his book *The Different Drum* (New York: Simon and Schuster, 1987) to refer to false communities in which people hide their concerns and disagreements behind masks of courtesy and respectability (86-90). False peace-keepers are those who encourage others to get along while preventing them from dealing with the fundamental issues that are pulling them apart. A true peace-maker is one who faces conflict, not one who covers it up. For real peace to happen, there must be more than a truce; the real reason for hostilities must be addressed, grievances must be aired, knowledge and understanding of the opposing positions must be acquired, and then there must be change, repentance and forgiveness on all sides, followed finally by healing and genuine community. This can not happen if false peace-keepers hinder the process by covering up the problems.

Unspoken rules. Another quote from the book: "In abusive spiritual systems, people's lives are controlled from the outside in by rules, spoken and unspoken. Unspoken rules are those that govern unhealthy churches or families, but are not said out loud" (67). In our church we have unspoken rules: We cannot say the prophet is too old. We cannot ask how much our leaders are paid. We will not hear told in general conference any stories about the historical practice of polygamy. The existence of unspoken rules is abusive because it engenders hypocrisy: we claim allegiance to one set of values, but we live by another.

In one case, the enforcement of an unspoken rule ended in the excommunication of an individual who challenged the stake president's mistaken understanding of common consent. The church law of common consent, as set forth in the revelations (D&C 20:60-67; 26:2; 28; 38:34-35; 41:9-11; 42:11; 102:9; 124:124-145) entitles members to vote any leader in and out of church office, regardless of whether the leader was called by revelation. But an unspoken rule of the church is that one is never to vote no, unless one has specific knowledge of wrongdoing, usually a sexual transgression, on the part of the leader whose name is presented. The stake president excommunicated this member for exercising his right to vote no without such specific knowledge, while apparently unaware of the teachings of church president Joseph F. Smith given in general conference in 1904:

> We desire that the Latter-day Saints will exercise the liberty wherewith they have been made free by the gospel of Jesus Christ; for they are entitled to know the right from the wrong, to see the truth and draw the line between it and error; and it is their privilege to judge for themselves and to act upon their own free agency with regard to their choice as to sustaining or otherwise those who should exercise the presiding functions among them. We desire the Latter-day Saints at this conference to exercise their prerogative, which is, to vote as the Spirit of the Lord prompts them on the measures and the men that may be presented to them (in Joseph F. Smith, *Gospel Doctrine* [Salt Lake City: Deseret Book Co., 1971], 48).

The "Can't Talk" rule. One particularly abusive unspoken rule deserves special mention: the "Can't Talk Rule," which may be stated best this way: If you bring up a problem, you become the problem (68). This rule contradicts the main assumption of the Restoration: if we are to receive greater light and knowledge, we must seek it. If Joseph Smith had not asked God which church was right, there would have been no Mormonism. Revelations come when they are sought. When people raise problems and issues, they are just asking questions. They are not denying authority; they are asking authority to do its job. And the answers authorities give do not end the discussion. They merely turn it in new directions and raise fresh questions. This is quite tedious work, and the best way to avoid it is to ignore questions, deny problems, and scapegoat those who raise them. This is effective, but highly abusive.

Other techniques. Johnson and VanVonderen list a number of other abusive techniques: the misuse of scripture, the demand that wives submit to husbands, the requirement that members just forgive and never confront abusers, the advice simply to ignore rather than deal with the past, the admonition to make checklists of dos and don'ts, the tactic of "bait and switch," and the technique of "triangulation" by which accusers refuse to confront the accused directly but only through some mediator. The authors also deal at length with the problem of false authority—authority based solely on ecclesiastical office and unrelated to love, truth, and spirituality.

Ecclesiastical tyranny. In addition to these abuses, some Mormons endure what I call ecclesiastical tyranny—the failure or refusal of church leaders to apply principles of fairness and due process in church administration or church courts, now called "disciplinary councils." The rules governing these councils are found in two places: the revelations (D&C 42, 102, 107, 121, 134) and in the church's *General Handbook of Instructions.* Unfortunately the procedural protections provided in the revelations are undermined in important ways by certain directives of the *Handbook.*

According to Doctrine and Covenants 102, members when disciplined by a high council are entitled to one-half the council to insure that the accused is not subjected to insult or injustice (v. 15). Two or more high councilors are to present the evidence (v. 13). The accused is entitled to an impartial judge (v. 20). The evidence is to be examined in its true light (v. 16). In cases where doctrine is at issue, the decision must be based on "sufficient writings"; if the case cannot be disposed of by this recourse, the president may seek revelation on the doctrine (v. 23). However, no person is ever to be judged by evidence obtained by revelation (*Teachings of the Prophet Joseph Smith,* 214). The general principles that govern the admissibility of evidence in a court of law apply in a disciplinary council, which includes the right of accuser, accused, and high councilors to call, examine, and cross-examine witnesses (*Gospel Doctrine,* 40; *Juvenile Instructor* 37 [15 Feb. 1902]: 114). Accuser and accused have the right to make closing statements (vv. 16-18). The stake presidency has the responsibility of formulating a tentative decision (v. 19), but only the high council can render that decision final by a majority vote (v. 22). The accused has a right to have the decision reconsidered (vv. 20-21) and, after reconsideration, to appeal the final decision to the First Presidency of the church (v. 26). If the accused is still not satisfied, Doctrine and Covenants 107 establishes a right of appeal to the general assembly of the priesthood quorums of the church (v. 32). From this there is but one more appeal, to the president of the High Priesthood plus twelve high priests acting as a court of last resort (v. 80). There are special procedures for trying a president of the church or of the high priesthood (vv. 32, 82, 83). No person is exempt from these procedures nor can they by any means be abridged (v. 84). I believe these procedures, when coupled with adequate notice and opportunity to prepare a defense, are sufficient to protect members from abuse in any disciplinary context. However, a number of the directives of the *General Handbook of Instructions* undermine these procedures. I will review only the most glaring procedural contradictions and problems.

Perhaps most disturbing is the tradition, reinforced by the *Handbook*, of according to Melchizedek priesthood holders the full procedural protections of scripture by ensuring them a hearing before the stake high council, while relegating non-Melchizedek priesthood holders, including adult women, to the less formal and less procedurally protected jurisdiction of the bishop's court. But even in a high council court setting the procedural protections of the revelations have been seriously eroded by the *Handbook*.

Another directive (*Handbook*, 10-2) requires the stake president or bishop to investigate the case. This directive conflicts with the requirement that the president or bishop be a judge and with the revelation of Doctrine and Covenants 102 that the judge be impartial. How can the judge be impartial if he is to weigh the evidence he himself has gathered? These directives require the bishop or stake president to act simultaneously in the conflicting roles as policeman, accuser, prosecutor, and judge—all of which are at odds with his role as pastor.

The *Handbook* (10-2) allows a bishop or stake president to ignore all the procedural safeguards if *informal* rather that than *formal* discipline is chosen by the leader. Informal discipline includes: private counsel/caution and informal probation, which can include indefinitely prohibiting the member from partaking of the sacrament, from holding church position, from attending the temple, from holding a temple recommend, etc. This directive does not protect a member from a bishop or stake president who may impose any of these deeply punitive sanctions unrighteously, or without adequate cause, or without sufficient evidence, or for improper reasons; nor does it take into account that members so disciplined are given no procedural recourse to correct abuses of the system.

Another directive prohibits bishops and stake presidents from giving to an accused member any specific information about the evidence that will be brought against the member in the disciplinary council (*Handbook*, 10-6). Moreover, the accused's witnesses may not attend the hearing together (10-7), while the accusers (who are often the members of the bishopric, stake presidency, or high council) are not prohibited from acting in concert against the accused. Other directives remove the final decision from the majority of the high council and rest it solely with the president of the stake (10-8), who, especially in cases of apostasy, is the individual usually bringing the charges.

The *Handbook* is at odds with the revelations, in part, because a confusion exists between the judicial functions of a high council and the governing functions of the Council of the Twelve. Though unanimity is required of the Twelve in reaching their decisions (D&C 107:27), there is nothing in the revelations that requires unanimity in the judicial decisions of a high council. If the high council does not act unanimously, this does not mean inspiration is lacking. The revelations do not allow the stake president to use his authority to manipulate a unanimous decision. To do so would render the participation of the high council a formality. The president is of course entitled to inspiration, but he is not entitled to have the last word. Only a majority of the high council may express the mind of the Lord in a disciplinary council (D&C 102:22). Nor may the high councilors abdicate this responsibility. In a church disciplinary council, unity is not the objective. Truth is the objective. And the majority rules. It should be reversible error to interpose procedures that violate this process or ignore it.

Perhaps the most treacherous mechanism of spiritual abuse in Mormonism is the use of a distorted concept of apostasy to prevent members from expressing their religious views. The dictionary definition of "apostasy" is rebellion against God or abandonment of one's faith. In the Old Testament it refers to Israel's unfaithfulness to God (see Jer. 2:19; 5:6; c.f. Josh. 22:22; 2 Chr. 33:19). In the New Testament it refers to the abandonment of Christian faith (see Heb. 6:6). Elder Bruce R. McConkie defined "apostasy" in *Mormon Doctrine* (Salt Lake City: Bookcraft, 1958) as the "abandonment and forsaking of . . . true principles" (41). All these are acceptable definitions for ordinary purposes, but no one of them could be used by a disciplinary council to determine if a member should be excommunicated or disfellowshipped. Many members lose or abandon their faith for various reasons. Some continue to attend church; others remain very involved with their faithful families and friends. Often we hold out hope that these individuals will return to full fellowship. Even though their "falling away" or "abandonment of faith" may technically be apostasy, church policy is, rightly, that they not be excommunicated, even if they join another (non-polygamist) church.

Excommunicable apostasy must be more than mere unbelief, more than disagreement, more even than dissension, contention, or opposition. To be excommunicable, apostasy must be to one's religion what treason is to one's country. To avoid condemning as apostasy mere lack of faith or differences of opinion, the formal definition of excommunicable apostasy must be carefully drafted so it does not have too wide a sweep. Fred Voros and I developed the following proposed definitional language:

> A member may be excommunicated for apostasy only upon proof of one or more of the following: (1) public renunciation of the divine authority of the Church of Jesus Christ of Latter-day Saints when accompanied by the commission of one or more overt acts intended to destroy the church, its members, or its property; or (2) perpetration of any criminal or fraudulent act intended to injure the church, its members, its property, or its reputation; or (3) the knowing and unauthorized creation or procurement, in whole or in part, of a new marriage contract, the knowing and unauthorized performance or procurement of the endowment ceremony, the knowing and unauthorized conferral of and ordination to priesthood office, or setting apart to church office; or (4) support of the apostate activities defined above given with the intent to destroy the church.

The purpose of this definition is to allow for a member's dissent, disagreement, disassociation, and even opposition, while permitting excommunication for only palpably injurious or destructive acts committed against the church. The proposal requires that excommunicable apostasy be proved by competent evidence, rather than by suppositions or feelings. Under part one of this proposal, a member could not be excommunicated simply for publicly or privately question-

ing or renouncing the church's claim to truth, divine authority, or inspiration unless the member could be shown to have
committed one or more overt acts intended to destroy the
church, its members, or its property. Thus a member's right
to doubt, disagree, disbelieve, and dissent would be protected. However, if the renunciation element of the definition could not be proved, a member could, nevertheless, be
excommunicated for perpetrating any criminal or fraudulent
acts intended to injure the church, its members, its property,
or its reputation. The injuries here, particularly to reputation, must be demonstrated and must result from a criminal
or fraudulent act, but not a tortious one (for example, slander
or libel). The purpose of this segment is to protect the church
from the criminal or fraudulent activities of members claiming to accept the truth of the church, while protecting such
members whose conduct falls short of crime or fraud. The
third segment of the definition allows the church to excommunicate members, whether they accept or reject the divine
authority of the church, if they either perform or procure an
ordination, endowment, or marriage sealing without proper
permission of the duly constituted leaders of the church. This
allows the church to expel members who perform without
permission those ordinances that create special relationships
of authority and power within the structure of the church.
Finally, to support, financially or otherwise, any of the afore-
mentioned apostate activities with intent to destroy the
church would also constitute proper grounds for excommunication.

   This proposal is very different from the church's current
three-part definition found in the *General Handbook of Instructions*—a definition that authorizes excommunications for any
reason or arguably no reason at all. Part one of the *Handbook*
definition makes excommunicable as apostasy an "act in

clear, open, and deliberate public opposition to the Church or its leaders" (10-3). Thus a member who makes an open or public statement may be excommunicated as an apostate if the church or any one of its leaders (local, regional, or general) considers the statement to be in opposition to that leader's views, even if the leader is acting in bad faith, illegally, under a mistake or misunderstanding, without proper authority, contrary to the established ordinances, revelations, or procedures of the church, or under circumstances where there is good reason for differences of opinion. This definition condemns as apostasy even courageous acts of faith, such as the open, deliberate, and loyal opposition of such individuals as Paul the apostle (Gal. 2:11-14), Samuel the Lamanite (3 Ne. 23), and even Jesus himself (Matt. 23).

Part two of the *Handbook* definition of excommunicable apostasy includes the "persistent teaching as Church doctrine of information that is not Church doctrine after members are corrected" by their bishops or high authority (10-3). Again the definition is too broad; for under it members who are merely mistaken or stubborn could be condemned as apostates. This is too harsh a punishment to impose upon persons who, though difficult, lack hostile intent and have committed no destructive acts. Moreover, much church doctrine is too elusive, inchoate, and controversial to serve as a standard for orthodoxy. Besides, the excommunication of mere dissenters would constitute an assault on personal liberty and a trespass on the human rights of members. Therefore, none of the following should be considered excommunicable apostasy: (1) speculating about church history, doctrine, or scripture; (2) maintaining, expressing, publishing, or speaking one's dissenting opinions; (3) believing (not practicing) or teaching (not intentionally supporting the practice of) a doctrine that is sincerely held, but questionable or even false (e.g., that there are people on the dark side of the moon and they dress like Quakers) or a doctrine that has been characterized by the church or its leaders as scripturally unsound, but which has historical, literary, or scientific support; (4) expressing personal differences with or even animosity toward church leaders—for to define the latter as apostasy is to value loyalty to church leaders over loyalty to God.

Part three of the *Handbook* definition condemns as excommunicable apostasy the "adherence by a member to the teachings of apostate cults (such as those that advocate plural marriage) after being corrected by bishops or higher authorities" (10-3). This definition is impossibly vague. The word cult is essentially a slur; any religion can be called a cult. The LDS church is regularly defamed in this way by anti-Mormons. This definition would arguably make excommunicable a person's membership in or support of a family if some of its members were polygamists. Excommunicable apostasy must be more than mere association in or involvement with a group. At the very least, it must be proved that the group is dedicated to the commission of specifically defined apostate acts; and then it must be shown that the accused member is a competent adult with control over his or her relationship to the group and is knowingly and intentionally involved as a supporter or perpetrator of its acts. To expel members without proving all of these elements is to promote a kind of Mormon McCarthyism—the punishment of people for mere associations that are either innocent, ill-advised, or coerced.

Why—in a church that has so much to offer and so many texts and traditions that contradict dominion, tyranny, and theological correctness—do we find so many examples of spiritual abuse? I believe the answer is faithlessness and fear.

There is a growing tendency for church leaders to reinterpret and preach the gospel in legalistic and judgmental terms, thereby undermining the Saints' faith in the unconditional love of Jesus Christ and his power to save. Moreover, there is fear—fear of impurity, fear of being contaminated with the things of the world, fear of being deceived, fear of displeasing God, fear of being persecuted or mocked. Our leaders, too, are afraid—afraid they will be held accountable for our sins, afraid they will fall short of their callings, afraid they will leave the church in worse condition than it was when it was put into their care.

These fears are very real. And to offset them, we anticipate our persecutors, our competitors, our detractors, and our critics. We try to avoid sin rather than to repent of it. We try to neutralize the effects of evil, real or imagined, even before the evil has occurred. We launch preemptive strikes. We engage in prior restraint.

In doing this we often objectify others, treating them as categories of evil rather than as individual persons with hopes and fears. In this way we manage to avoid their personhood altogether and deal with them as enemies, or apostates, or anti-Mormons, or liberals, right-wingers, fundamentalists, or intellectuals. Thus we nullify them as people. We do not have to be influenced by them. We do not have to consider what they say, or if they are in pain, or if we have caused that pain. We can just banish them from our world view altogether. We can make them nonpersons. As the Book of Mormon says, we "notice them not" (Morm. 8:39). This is a terrible temptation. Especially for a people who themselves have been objectified as enemies, non-Christian, cultist, foolish, and anti-intellectual. If Mormonism has become closed and repressive, it may be because it was the object of persecution and abuse. As D. Michael Quinn has observed about our

Mormon history, those who have been abused often grow to be abusive to others. If we perceive ourselves as victims, always victims, then we can always justify as self-defense our abusive treatment of others. This is understandable but wrong. Those who have been abused in the past are only postponing the moment of their own healing by repaying those abuses with further abuse in the present. What we need is to understand our fears, our pain, our deep resentments and hurts—and the fears, pain, resentment, and hurts of others. Knowledge is the doorway to spirituality. It is to this end that God gives us spiritual gifts. Prophecy, revelation, instruction, inspiration, insight, even the gifts of healing and tongues were given, not to prove that we are right, but to give us understanding of ourselves and others, so that we might love others as we are loved by God. Fear arises upon ignorance. Love arises upon knowledge. Without knowledge and understanding there can be no love, no hope, no joy. Knowing others requires that we listen to them, respect them, deal with them in justice, fairness, mercy, compassion, and hope. Only in such climate can we open our hearts to each other. This is not to say that there is no place for anger or reproof or criticism, but these things must be mutual and reciprocal, and there must exist adequate procedures for dealing with dissent, disagreement, discord, and disputation. Power must never be used to favor one over another, only to assure a level playing for all. We need not be neutral, but we must be even-handed. The fact that we are full of passionate convictions should not disable us from accommodating the convictions and passions of others, even if they are quite different from our own. Every right we claim for ourselves, we must willingly accord to our detractors. And for every control we impose on others, we must be willing to have a like control imposed on us. Only by engaging in this kind of reciprocity can we understand the wisdom of creating as few controls and prohibitions as possible in order to maximize self-determination, self-definition, and self-actualization. We must not interfere too much in the spiritual journeys of others. If we prevent people from making mistakes, we prevent them from spiritual growth. This is, in part, the meaning of Jesus' statement: Do unto others as you would have them do unto you.

Unfortunately, many of us are too hurt, too fearful, too exhausted even to desire understanding and knowledge. We can love those who are like us, but not those who are different. We are convinced that our pain and our sorrow is worse and our views, our assumptions, and our aspirations are better than anyone else's. We defend our insularity, our xenophobia, our elitism, our narcissism as purity. In the name of keeping our doctrine pure, our church pure, our traditions pure, we ignore the pleas and criticisms of others and turn ever more inward, clinging ever more fiercely to our obsession that we, we few, we band of brothers, we alone are God's chosen, we alone are his people, we alone are the elect. And thus, by imperceptible degrees are we led carefully into idolatry, in which we prize self-love above charity, self-help above sacrifice, self-aggrandizement above spirituality, self-atonement above Christ's atonement, and self-praise above the praise of God.

I have said all this in other ways in other places. Talking about these things is important. We must continue to talk. But we must also act both to promote what is good and to oppose what is bad in Mormonism. And to this end the Mormon Alliance was organized as a non-profit corporation on 4 July 1992. The date has no political significance. It is not an organization about politics either of the left, the center, or the right. Its mission and purpose is to uncover, identify, define, name, chronicle, resist, and even combat acts and threats of defamation and spiritual abuse perpetrated on Mormon individuals and institutions by Mormon and non-Mormon individuals and institutions. Within the Alliance there are four major divisions: the Reconciliation Committee, the Defense Committee, the Case Reports Committee, and the Common Consent Committee.

A. The Reconciliation Committee opens and maintains a correspondence with the leadership of the church on issues of importance to the Alliance.

B. The Defense Committee acts to contradict anti-Mormon sentiments and in a constructive way assist in defending the church, its leaders, and its members from libel, slander, and defamation by non-Mormon individuals or institutions.

C. The Case Reports Committee compiles, verifies, and publishes accounts of defamation and spiritual abuse and the courageous acts of individuals working to resist spiritual abuse.

D. The Common Consent Committee promotes principles of justice, fairness, even-handedness, equity, and due process in the treatment of Mormon individuals and institutions by other Mormon individuals and institutions.

The Mormon Alliance is about change. I believe in change. We are changed by birth, by life, by rebirth, and by death. Our eschatology tells us that when Christ comes the whole world order will be changed. I believe this too—the strange teaching that the trumpet shall sound and the dead shall be raised incorruptible, and that we shall all be changed. The yoke of the oppressor shall be lifted. The haughty shall be humbled, and the hearts of the hardened, broken. The old, corrupt world of greed, power, lust, and abuse, shall be made new again. The lamb and the lion shall lie down together without any ire, and Ephraim be crowed with his blessings in Zion, and Jesus descend in his chariot of fire. Yes, we shall all be changed. I believe the time for change is upon us. Those who choose now to advance it must be bold and courageous, willing to take risks, willing to suffer abuse, discouragement, and loss. Nevertheless, I believe that those who make this effort with purity of heart will have the blessing and help of the Almighty and will find, in the end, that they have played some small part in strengthening the Saints and in helping the church to receive the healing spirituality that today—in this hour of darkness—is our most pressing need.

Chapter Eight.

THE SANCTITY OF DISSENT

"The Sanctity of Dissent" was originally delivered to the B. H. Roberts Society in Salt Lake City, Utah, on 13 May 1993.

I wish here to explain why I think dissent should be embraced by the church as holy—that is, inspired and ordained of God as necessary to the spiritual well-being of the church.

To dissent is to differ in sentiment or opinion, to disagree with the philosophy, methods, or goals of others, especially the majority. It is to withhold one's assent. Dissent is almost always disruptive. It can be dangerous, even violent. There exist forms of dissent as acceptable as casting a ballot, as provocative as crossing a boundary, as intolerable as terrorism or hate crimes. Moreover, the purposes of dissent may range from the sublimely noble to the utterly contemptible. Clearly, a community need not endure every manifestation of dissent.

Nevertheless, dissent, in its essence, is holy. Jesus himself was a dissenter, and this fact alone hallows dissent. "Think not," he said, "that I am come to send peace on earth: I came not to send peace, but a sword" (Matt. 10:34). The sword is asserted here not as a metaphor for physical violence, but as the cruciform symbol of opposition. The cutting edge of contrary opinion can divide a complacent community, challenging its received wisdom and settled opinions. Actual physical confrontation, though sometimes necessary, is not essential. The essence of dissent—that is, dissent stripped of any specific form or context—is the fundamental right to disagree and to express that disagreement. In this essay when I speak of dissent, I mean this essential freedom of opposition. In the first part of this essay I will discuss ten reasons why I believe dissent is sacred; later I will show how dissent is further sanctified by the adoption of certain means and objectives.

*Dis*sent is holy because without it there can be no *con*sent. Consent is a voluntary meeting of the minds. It is the agreement of free individuals who share a perception of what is mutually beneficial or at least acceptable to them. Consent is meaningful only where dissent is permitted and protected. Consent draws its power from the possibility of dissent. Unless the consenting parties are free to dissent, their consent is without substance and pointless. Thus if dissent is proscribed, assent is illusory. Like a fascist election, it is a counterfeit—a fraud—because behind it there is no true accord. To eliminate dissent, then, is to curtail personal freedom, to forbid individuals from voicing their true opinions. It is to silence both their hopes and their fears. It is to force people to accept what they deem unacceptable, even harmful. By eliminating dissent, a community takes from its members the power to resist or contradict. It neutralizes opposition by abridging an individual's right to protest, to object, to cry out in pain. Such a system is a prison in which every act of kindness may be an exploitation; and every act of love, a rape.

Dissent is holy because it is the backbone of individual freedom, the freedom from arbitrary compulsion. Any proscription of dissent is an attack on this hallowed principle. Such attacks are being made by church leaders at all levels. The prevailing view of the current leadership is that we are free only to choose what is good. "After all," the argument goes, "the commandments are clear. There are prophets to guide us. Why be free, when you can be right?" This is the most succinct summation of the salvation plan of compulsion scripturally attributed to Satan as I ever expect to hear.

Goodness, however, does not result from obedience, even obedience to someone good. It results from spiritual transformation, a change of heart, a rebirth. Goodness is personal spiritual maturity. We cannot mature spiritually if we are under compulsion, if we are required to yield to others the responsibility for our words and deeds. Goodness results from turning our hearts to God, from listening to the voice of God within our hearts, within the hearts of our family and friends, within the hearts of all the concerned members of our religious community. We cannot be free and slavishly follow a prescribed catechism. We cannot be organization men and women. We must work out our own salvation, not with smugness and certainty, but "with fear and trembling" (Philip. 2:12).

Dissent is holy because it is essential to salvation. Adam and Eve dissented in Eden as a necessary step toward spiritual growth. Christ's dissent led him to the cross and beyond. A child dissents when he or she follows the scriptural admonition to "leave father and mother" (Gen. 2:24). An adult dissents whenever he or she exercises independent judgment or personal initiative. Jesus intended for us to dissent. He said,

> I am come to set a man at variance against his father, and the daughter against her mother, and the daugh-

ter in law against her mother in law. A man's foes shall be they of his own household. He that loveth father or mother more than me is not worthy of me: and he that loveth son or daughter more than me is not worthy of me. And he that taketh not his cross, and followeth after me, is not worthy of me (Matt. 10:35-38).

Hard words from the Prince of Peace. They mean that essential to salvation is the sacred freedom to dissent from the wisdom of the group—the family, the church, the state—in order to be true to the wisdom of God. Easy to say. That is why so many find it easier simply to consent, even when consent is cajoled or coerced. Many such members are fond of saying of the church to their dissenting brothers and sisters: "Love it or leave it." These souls cannot accept the possibility that the church might be wrong, might be headed toward idolatry. But it can. It always has in the past. And it always will. The church is no purer than its members. It can sin. And it can also be corrected and improved, not just by leaders, but by members who take responsibility for its health, spirituality, and well-being. In defense of dissent, Brigham Young once said: "Now when I was an Elder I was as willing to correct an error in the Brethren as I am now. But the people do not see it so. Now if you should be with the 12 or any body you would have a right to correct an error as well as with a member but you could not correct them by cutting them off from the church because they are over you in the priesthood" (in Wilford Woodruff's journal, 2 June 1857, LDS archives). The Doctrine and Covenants urges every member to cry repentance to his or her generation. What is such a cry, but the voice of dissent?

Dissent is holy because it is the root of personal responsibility and spiritual maturation. Without dissent, self-determination is not possible. Only those who are free to disagree with the prevailing views of the group can learn the full implications of their personal views. Only those free to dissent can fully take part in the decision-making processes that shape their lives and destinies. Only they, by participating in the governing decisions of the group, can experience spiritual and intellectual development. For this reason, dissent is an indispensable component of every moral organization dedicated to the empowerment and salvation of the individual. A system that punishes dissent thwarts personal growth, perpetuates childishness, and promotes arrested adolescence. It will come, eventually, to value compliance and obedience above the personal sanctity of its members. In such a system individuals will be valued only if they repress their personal spiritual insights in the interest of conformity. Those who do not or cannot comply will be scapegoated or marginalized. Such a system will urge or even compel its members to live by principles they do not truly value and to submit to values they do not truly accept. Inevitably such a system will become joyless and unforgiving in its denial of the truth. It will become evil.

Dissent is holy because it is essential to continuing, personal revelation. The most vital role of revelation is to initiate change, correction, reproof, not to reinforce the status quo. To eliminate dissent, then, is to risk silencing the "still small voice" of the holy spirit speaking to us the discourse of dissent. Though Mormonism is based on the concept of continuing revelation, the church does not accept God as dissenter, in spite of his incarnation as a rebellious rabbi. The argument against the sanctity of dissent goes like this: "The church is not a democracy. It is a theocracy. It is governed by God through his chosen prophets and apostles. When we sustain them, we give our consent, we agree to obey our leaders because they have been chosen by God and are inspired to know what is best for us." This view contradicts the weight of scripture and religious experience. Prophets do not always speak as prophets. Prophecy is a spiritual gift, not an office. Contact with God is uncertain at best, even for the best of us. Jesus said, "The wind bloweth where it listeth, and thou hearest the sound thereof, but canst not tell whence it cometh, and whither it goeth; so is every one that is born of the Spirit" (John 3:8).

Salvation and spirituality are like the wind—real but uncertain, powerful but outside human control. It is improper for the church to insist that our authorized leaders may be relied upon with certainty. This assertion wrongly suggests that members may rely upon the church and its leaders for salvation. But the church is not the source of salvation. The church is what needs to be saved. Salvation is God's work, not our work. In scripture God states emphatically, "This is *my* work and *my* glory—to bring to pass the immortality and eternal life of [men and women]" (Moses 1:39).

Unfortunately, divine salvation seems fairly unpredictable to many of us. We long for certainty, for security, for safety. And the institutional church is all too willing to assume the burden of providing these. Individuals are encouraged to follow the Spirit in the process of conversion or reactivation; but once in the fold, they are told to "follow the Brethren." Inspiration and revelation are then limited to the variety that confirms that leaders are right or, even if wrong, that they are to be obeyed. In this way, the church establishes itself as the principle agent of salvation and in doing so contravenes such warnings as: "Trust not in the arm of flesh" (D&C 1:19), and "I am the Lord thy God . . . thou shalt have no other gods before me" (Ex. 20:2-3). The church cannot substitute for the Spirit of God, because the church has no divine power to heal us, forgive us, redeem us, resurrect us, exalt us, or fill us with the love that is stronger than the cords of death. The church does, of course, have a divine role: to encourage repentance and forgiveness, to mitigate fear, foster faith, raise hope, and promote charity. But it can do this only if it permits dissent. If it prohibits dissent, it will undercut its divine role and relegate itself to the profane business of hawking self-improvement schemes and motivating material success. Its main mission will be limited to the production of respectable citizens who make good employees rather than Saints, and fine family members rather than friends of God.

Mormonism without dissent is what Hugh Nibley calls "world's fair Mormonism," what Michael Quinn calls, "cookie cutter Mormonism," and what I call "McMormonism, or fast food Mormonism." The McMormon church favors sin avoidance over repentance, purity over holiness, and morality over mystery. Preachments focus on safety—safety from the "thousand natural shocks that flesh is heir to" (*Hamlet* III, i, 62-63), safety from the very experiences of life that, as premortal spirits, we are said to have been so anxious to encounter as essential to the attainment of wisdom. By quashing dissent the modern church discourages members from relying on the voice of the Spirit in their hearts and encourages them to rely on idols, both sacred and secular, both living and dead.

Dissent is holy because it is an antidote to idolatry. The essence of idolatry is to mistake the part for the whole, to see as simple what is complex. The divine nature is whole and dynamic, while the symbols, texts, rituals, and myths of the divine are, in comparison, incomplete and static. When the corporate church fixes the attention of its members on these lesser constructs rather than the greater, it begins to distance them from authentic worship. When this happens, the voice of God is muted in the ecclesiastical institution, but it continues to speak a discourse of dissent through the church's loyal critics. The prohibition of dissent in such times facilitates idolatry. It stimulates the adulation of authority, priesthood, church affiliation, theology, scripture, rules, and traditions rather than the worship of God. Brigham Young said:

> What is commonly termed idolatry has arisen from a few sincere men, full of faith and having a little knowledge, urging upon a backsliding people to preserve some customs—to cling to some fashions or figures, to put them in mind of that God with whom their fathers were acquainted . . . Idols have been introduced . . . to preserve among the people the idea of the true God (*Journal of Discourses* 6:194).

Idolatry is the invention of well-meaning persons attempting to preserve some semblance of faith. It is often promoted in the name of spiritual certitude or purity. But a truly religious life is not one of certainty, security, or safety. No fixed patterns or formulas were meant to work for everyone. The spiritual journey is tailor-made for the individual taking it. It is through the instrumentality of dissent that idolatry is contradicted, the personal dimension of religion restored, and the right of each individual to worship God according to the dictates of his or her own conscience preserved.

Dissent is holy because it gives sight to the blind. A system that proscribes dissent blinds itself. There are many kinds of sight: foresight, insight, hindsight. Perhaps the most valuable is ironic sight. Usually, we think of irony as sarcasm, but it has a broader literary meaning: irony is the technique of seeing or communicating two or more meanings in a single utterance. In a religious context ironic vision is the vision that sees simultaneously the natural and the supernatural, the spiritual and the physical, the sacred and the profane, the cosmic and the mundane, that sees in a symbol, event, or experience various levels of meaning at once, that sees ourselves as others see us. Ironic vision allows us to escape the prison of our egos and view our lives and relationships from new and differing perspectives. To see ourselves as we are seen by those who employ us and whom we employ, by those who depend on us and on whom we depend, by those who teach and learn from us, who lead and follow us, who love and hate us. To see from these shifting perspectives is probably one of the most repentance-inducing experiences any individual can have. This may be the greatest, if not least valued, of the spiritual gifts.

A religious system that proscribes dissent, that requires its members to accept the party-line on all important questions contrary to their true feelings, robs its members of ironic vision. Introspection will become more and more difficult. Individuals will find themselves increasingly unable to see the world, their organization, themselves, or their relationships from the vantage point of other members or of non-members of their group. Specifically, without ironic vision in the church, individual Mormons will not be inclined to ask important questions: How is the LDS church in its second century like the Christian church in its second century? How is the current leadership and membership of the church responsible for the continued practice of polygamy by Mormon fundamentalists? How do others view us when we brag about our living prophet, and then show them the actual condition of the president of the church? What does the church look and feel like from the point of view of a conservative? a widow? a survivalist? a bishop? a divorcee? a troubled teenager? a homosexual? a high councilor? an apostle? an apostle's wife? In the absence of dissent, members will have little impetus to ask: What are the church's problems? What causes those problems? What must be done to eliminate those problems? The Old Testament proverb states: "Where there is no vision, the people perish" (Prov. 29:18). Dissent is crucial to this very vision.

Dissent is holy because it can also heal institutional blindness. In the New Testament, Jesus accuses the Pharisees of blindness as if it were a sin (Matt. 23). I used to be confused by this denunciation. Why should Jesus treat blindness as sin? Blindness is a sin when it is self-inflicted by those who do not wish to see the sins they have committed or enabled, who do not wish to see their own pain and suffering, or the pain and suffering they have caused others. This type of blindness is denial. It is the ultimate mechanism of control to which abusers retreat when their abuses are exposed. Self-inflicted blindness may be institutionalized. Institutions do this by punishing truth telling and rewarding the denial or repression of truth. This cannot happen in an institution, unless there exist individual leaders willing to enforce such punishments and rewards.

How are such accomplices identified and empowered in the church? By the following mechanism: First, the leadership of the church must be stratified into descending classes of power: First Presidency, Council of the Twelve, First Quorum of Seventy, right down to the bishops and quorum presidents. Then rules, spoken and unspoken, must be developed to govern each of these groups and, more importantly, an individual's advancement from one of these groups to another. If an individual is to move into a higher strata of leadership—with its increased power, privileges, and tenure—he must demonstrate not only obedience to all church policies, but political correctness and acumen in recognizing and submitting to the personal views of the top brass. To advance one must "anticipate counsel," to use the phrase of one general authority. Thus only the truly correlated may ascend to the inner circles of leadership, with all their benefits and rewards. The system ensures that only those juniors who have become faithful replicas of their seniors will participate in the most important decisions of the leadership elite.

This is precisely the system that was employed by Soviet premier Leonid Brezhnev to ensure the stability of communism in the Soviet Union. For this reason, I refer to this system in Mormonism as the Brezhnevization of the church. Its problem, however, is that it not only screens out the uncorrelated and undesirable, it also screens out the capable and creative. In the Soviet Union, the leadership became incapable of responding to the needs of the people or of the group. Corruption and incompetence crippled the country. The leadership responded to criticism by becoming evermore rigid and authoritarian. Finally, compelled by desperate circumstances, the leadership had no other choice than to make concessions. This was like putting a crack in an already weakened and swollen dam. The internal pressures caused a breach and a flood that no amount of renewed authoritarianism could avert or contain. The problem with rewarding consent and punishing dissent is that it causes self-inflicted blindness that deprives the institution of vision, ironic or otherwise. Dissent is holy because it is, perhaps, the only corrective to institutional blindness, the only means of giving to its blind members insight, foresight, and hindsight into perspectives to which their minds would otherwise be closed. Dissent is holy because, even if the blind refuse to see, its purpose is to prepare against the hour of disaster, when the blind lead the blind into a ditch.

MT. LEBANON PUBLIC LIBRARY

Dissent is holy because it is the foundation of peace. Though the principal reason for the elimination of dissent is to avoid discord and disruption, the elimination of dissent does not promote peace. Instead, the absence of dissent is evidence of unspoken turmoil hidden by repression, suppression, or oppression. Yes, dissent is noisy. And some feel dissent should be silenced in the interest of tranquility. But tranquility is not peace. Silence is not peace. In fact, silence when imposed by the strong on the weak is one of the most efficient mechanisms of control. The first act of physical, sexual, or spiritual abusers is to silence their victims. Real peace is based on freedom, authenticity, and love. These cannot flower in the inhospitable climate of suppression and repression. We should not listen to those who cry "peace, peace," when there is no peace—when peace is merely a euphemism for subjugation. The Book of Mormon admonition, "Wo be unto him that is at ease in Zion! Wo be unto him that crieth: All is well!" (2 Ne. 28:24-25), warns us to avoid confusing peace with its counterfeits: politeness, pseudo-community, feigned love, and the comfortable familiarity of the status quo.

Dissent is holy because it safeguards the community from self-destruction. To eliminate dissent is to doom the organization. Unless the discourse of dissent is permitted, protected, and encouraged, an organization has no way to test the adequacy of its decisions to meet the problems of the group. It has no way to assure that its policies accord with spiritual truth, with natural reality, or with the needs of its members. Only by allowing dissent to be expressed and to accumulate support on the basis of merit alone can a group be assured that its decisions are made in light of the experience of all its concerned members rather than the limited experience of its leadership enclave. Of course, there are problems with democratic governance. The majority almost never has the technical knowledge possessed by an expert minority; and the wisdom of the majority is by no means infallible. This is precisely the point. What is necessary to protect the community from both the wrongheadedness of the multitude and the narrow-mindedness of the elite is a courageous and loyal opposition. When the wisdom of the many and the prudence of the few fail, an organization is most likely to find the vitality and vision to survive in the voices of its dissenting members.

Let me now discuss briefly seven means and objectives that can add to the sanctity of dissent: Dissent is hallowed when its objective is the eradication of evil. Many of us do not believe in evil. Or if we do we see it as only illusory or superficial. Many do not believe in evil people, evil groups, or evil systems. This view informed England prior to World War II. Many Britons believed Hitler was not evil, merely misunderstood, and that it was possible to make peace with him. This view obtained even after the Anschluss of Austria, the attack on Czechoslovakia, and the invasion of Poland. For those who do not believe in evil, there seems little justification for dissent. The holiest dissent, with all its discord and cantankerousness, is asserted to oppose evil, to expose evil, to resist evil. I believe in the reality of evil. But, for me, evil is something quite specific: it is the persistent or systematic abuse of power by the strong to the detriment of the weak. Evil in this sense can corrupt individuals and institutions. The church is not exempt. Within its divinely authorized structures, evil can and does manifest itself as spiritual abuse, which I have defined and discussed in other places.

Evil must not be confused with one's personal sins. I am not here calling for personal perfection in leaders or in members. I understand that everyone is susceptible to foolishness, bad judgment, contrariness, selfishness, and sin. These are not the issue. They should not be confused with spiritual abuse. Spiritual abuse is systemic. It is a sin of relationship. It is a community sin. Church leaders who commit spiritual abuse do so not simply because they are imperfect, but because they hold a false concept of authority which is shared by the membership. When church leaders perpetrate spiritual abuse, it is only because church members enable them to do so. Let me emphasize that it is dangerous to permanently stigmatize any person or institution as evil. This too is an abuse. Notwithstanding, it is critical to see that the heart of darkness, the soul of evil, is the deliberate perpetuation and exploitation of powerlessness by the strong, often with the complicity of the weak. The antidote to such unhallowed control is the sanctity of dissent.

Dissent is further sanctified when its substance is truth. Truth telling is the holiest discourse of dissent. But truth telling is hard. We do not deal in truth directly. We deal in shifting perceptions of truth. Our knowledge, whether attained by study or by faith, whether sacred or secular, is incomplete, limited, inaccurate, and flawed. We see through a glass darkly. Different people see the same events and hear the same words differently. Intentions are often misunderstood. The same facts give rise to differing conclusions depending upon one's assumptions, convictions, intentions, and expectations. Each of us is flawed and often disposed to manage or mismanage the truth in our own interest. In the hands of controlling people, truth becomes a terrible weapon.

For all these reasons, authentic truth-tellers must first search their own hearts for and rid themselves of any inclination to be self-serving, or to perpetuate or exploit the weak, even if the weak seem to deserve it, even if the weak have the outward appearance of being strong. Truth telling requires us to face and admit our own weaknesses, shortcomings, and sins. As truth tellers we must be willing to reveal our own lack of knowledge, flawed logic, faulty intuitions, misunderstandings, inexperience, fears, doubts, fantasies, false hopes, egotistical dreams, and uninformed or unsettled opinions. We must be willing to confess the abuses we have perpetrated or enabled and to acknowledge how we have been controlled, compelled, and dominated by others. We must make these disclosures at the proper level of abstraction. It will not do for us to reveal the abuses of others with great specificity and then to relate our own with great generality.

In other words, we must not only be forthright but even-handed, not only factually accurate but intellectually honest. Our motives and agendas must be clear. We cannot allow ourselves to hide our hurt, our pain, our anger behind façades of composure and value neutral rhetoric. Disinformation and nondisclosure merely postpone the moment of truth. If we wish to tell the truth, we must be willing to make fools of ourselves, rather than to cover our sins, gratify our pride, and deflect humiliation. Our stories must be without melodrama, without romantic excess, without flawless characters, without deceptions. We must accept that, as truth tellers, we will often appear politically incorrect and less astute than our opponents.

Our dissent is further sanctified when we take seriously the views of others. Dissent, if it is to be effective, must follow the golden rule. It must treat others as it would be treated. It must listen, even when its opposition is unpleasant, confused, discordant, and controlling. We cannot be like those in the free-speech movement of the 1960s who, in the interest of the cause of free speech, suppressed the speech of their opponents. Listening is not easy. There is always the temptation to stop listening, to be defensive, to protect ourselves, to anticipate rejection by rejecting others first. Dissent does not allow us to withdraw from others. Dissent is to criticize, not to trivialize. True dissent is not possible if we associate only with those who are like us, who comfort us, who tell us what we want to hear. We cannot truly dissent if we cease to hear our loyal opposition. Dissent is holiest when it treats the views of others as it wishes its own views to be treated.

Dissent is further sanctified when it promotes genuine community. By telling truth and listening to truth, we come to terms with our own experiences of abuse and the experiences of others; we breakdown façades; we take responsibility for our personal and our community shadows. Through dissent we provide each other with the common bread of authenticity and the common cup of charity. However, to take responsibility is not to take blame. No person can assume the culpability for the freely chosen beliefs, acts, and words of others. Those who do will invariably try to impose righteousness to avoid this vicarious guilt. Too many church leaders think this way. But leaders are not responsible for the wrongs of members; nor can members avoid personal responsibility by blindly following leaders. We are, however, all responsible for the well-being of the church.

Such responsible dissent possesses the spiritual power to awaken consciousness, raise awareness, create paradigms, alter opinions, heal wounds, and bring wholeness and holiness to our community. But it must be remembered that dissent raises the stakes. It is by nature confrontational. Even when carefully and artfully advanced, truth telling and dissent are usually not well-received. One of the recurring mistakes of my life has been my silly belief that I would somehow endear myself to others by telling them what I believe to be the truth. Jesus, however, did not say that the truth would make us well-liked. He said that "the truth shall make you free" (John 8:32). What he did not say was that it would first make everybody madder than hell.

But this is just another reason why dissent is holy: it fosters accountability. To tell the truth is to call to account, to call to repent. This is unpleasant business. It invites reciprocity. It invites calls to repentance to be levelled in return. When this happens, we must listen to each other. If we do not, we risk entering a vicious cycle of mutual distrust and backbiting that will postpone healing. Confrontation is often necessary to break this vicious cycle, especially if abusive individuals respond to calls to account with denial, with self-inflicted blindness. In such instances, confrontation is to dissenters what a scalpel is to a surgeon: it inflicts the wounds that heal. Nevertheless, hurt feelings may be lessened if our call is not petty, trivial, or mean-spirited—if the discourse of dissent is not directed against personal short-comings, petty sins, and pet peeves—but in favor of liberty and love and against the perpetuation or exploitation of powerlessness.

Dissent is sanctified when it is sacrificial, tactful, hopeful, charitable, clear, courageous, and grace-filled. Jesus cautioned us to be as wise as serpents and as harmless as doves. Those church members who dissent vocally or publicly must be prepared for criticism and censure, for accusations of impurity, impiety, and impropriety, for charges of unchristianlike conduct and apostasy. They must be prepared to lose their temple recommends, to be disfellowshipped, and to be excommunicated. Let there be no mistake, these are highly punitive actions which, if not administered with the utmost care and the utmost consideration for fairness and due process, become acts of abuse and even violence. Nevertheless, when these abuses come, dissent is made holier if abused dissenters do not become heartless, reckless, or cruel; if they face abuse without returning abuse; if they remain fair and forthright in the face of denial; if they rely on the inner strength and authorization of the Holy Spirit when abandoned by family, friends, co-workers, neighbors, fellow members and when threatened with the loss of jobs, careers, and financial security. Clearly, dissent is not for everyone, nor is it necessary that everyone dissent. For this reason, too, dissent is holy: it is a spiritual vocation. Not all are called. But those who are will probably not find peace or spiritual fulfillment in any other way.

There is one more reason I believe dissent to be holy. It is, perhaps, the most important of all. I will make my point with a story: In 1412, there was born to French peasants of Domremy-la-Pucell, a girl—Jeanne to the French, Joan to us. When she was twelve, she began to see and hear in vision St. Michael, St. Catherine, and St. Margaret. In 1429, during the Hundred Years' War, just when the English were about to capture Orléans, Joan was exhorted by these heavenly beings to save France. She presented herself to the king and a board of theologians approved her claims. At the age of seventeen and with no experience of combat, she—clad in armor, mounted on a charger, and holding aloft a white banner emblazoned with the fleur-de-lis (the symbol of God's grace)— led the French in battle after battle to a stunning and decisive victory against the English. At the dauphin's coronation she held the place of honor beside him. Later, King Charles withdrew his support for further campaigns, but Joan continued, engaging the English at Compiègne, near Paris. There, captured by Burgundian soldiers, she was sold to the English, who turned her over to an ecclesiastical court at Rouen to be tried for heresy and sorcery. She underwent fourteen months of interrogation. She was accused of consorting with demons, of wearing a man's apparel, and of insubordination. But her most seditious crime, her most heinous sin was that she believed that she was directly responsible to God and not to the Catholic church. She penitently confessed herself a sinner and was sentenced to life imprisonment rather than to death. But once in prison, she set aside the counsels of the church and, in direct response to the revelations of God, resumed wearing men's clothes. For this she was condemned as a relapsed heretic and, on the 30th day of May of 1431, in the Old Market Square of Rouen, Joan of Arc was burned at the stake. Twenty-five years later, the church retried her case and proclaimed her innocent. In 1920 she was canonized St. Joan by Pope Benedict XV. Dissent is holy because it requires us to be ultimately responsible not to any earthly power, but to God directly.

I know that what I am saying now will not touch some of you. Some have lost faith in Mormonism. Some have no faith in spiritual callings or religious ideals. The pain and disillusionment have been too great. I have no judgment for you. I hope you have none for me. But the current state of our faith does not matter. God, whose grace is sufficient for us, can raise even our lost faith from the dead. What matters now is that we acknowledge to ourselves the evil and abuse that are occurring all around us in our community; that we accept that the heartache of its victims is real; that their pain is real; that in our church the dysfunction, the breakdown of faith, the loss of hope, the rejection of love are all real; and that real, too, is the long litany of our community sins: pride, compulsion, egotism, and fear.

Earlier, I said that the sword is the cruciform symbol of dissent against cruelty, corruption, unhallowed control, against denial, false peace, and forced silence. Jesus spoke the discourse of divine dissent against such evils in history.

The Holy Ghost continues in the present to speak this same discourse in the hearts of many of us. Those who hear that voice, the voice of one crying in the wilderness, must give up all hope of banal material success, must take up—not the sword—but the cross and, like St. Joan, find sanctuary in the sanctity of dissent.

Chapter Nine.

ALL IS NOT WELL IN ZION: FALSE TEACHINGS OF THE TRUE CHURCH

"All Is Not Well in Zion: False Teachings of the True Church"
was originally a presentation given at the Sunstone Theological
Symposium in August 1993. This speech, together with my re-
sponses to the questions of the stake presidency and high council of
the Salt Lake Big Cottonwood Stake concerning it, served as the sole
evidentiary basis for my excommunication from the church on 19
September 1993.

"Wo be unto him that is at ease in Zion! Wo be unto him that
crieth: All is well!" (2 Ne. 28:24-25) This scripture, familiar to
students of the Book of Mormon, warns that trouble, distress,
and affliction—perhaps even divine judgment—await those
who are at ease in Zion, who are comfortable in their knowledge, power, wealth, and connections, who have a stake in
the status quo, who are prospering, who are secure (see 2 Ne.
28:21). There are many in the LDS church, of course, who
would argue that this text does not apply to us or to our time,
but to someone somewhere and somewhen else. To say this,

however, is to fall into the snare of the text. If we are not made uneasy by this text, then we define ourselves as those who are "at ease in Zion"—and wo unto us. If, on the other hand, we accept that the text's warning applies to us, if we let it reveal our uncertainty and dis/ease, then the text can work upon us. It can move us to repent and forgive, to mature into spiritual beings of compassion and truth.

One of the stunning paradoxes of Jesus is that those of us who are most certain of our righteousness are likely to be farthest from the divine, from the attributes of love, compassion, justice, truth, vitality, authenticity, and holiness, while those in trouble, distress, and affliction, those who feel torn between the holy and the profane may indeed be in the womb of the Holy Spirit, suffering with God the labor of their own spiritual rebirth.

Even now the evidence of Zion's sickness proliferates. The Mormon Alliance is documenting dozens of cases in which certain abuses are being repeatedly perpetrated by church leaders, not just on intellectuals, but on all categories of Latter-day Saints throughout the worldwide church. Members are being called in and threatened with disciplinary action simply because they have engaged in public or private discussions of religious and/or church-related topics. Leaders are regularly using the temple recommend and, in the case of Brigham Young University students, the ecclesiastical endorsement procedures arbitrarily to coerce members' compliance not to the teachings of the church but to the private views of individual leaders. Increasing numbers of stake presidents and bishops are employing disciplinary procedures that are inconsistent with those set forth in the Doctrine and Covenants and with fundamental principles of fairness and due process. General authorities continue to maintain secret files on and to conduct surveillance of nonviolent church members, to instruct local leaders to tell members that an inquiry into the member's church standing originated at the local level when in fact it did not, and to withhold from members information on such issues as church finances, history, and decision-making. Church leaders at all levels foster, as a matter of policy, the concept that power or influence may be maintained by priesthood authority alone, without persuasion, long-suffering, gentleness, meekness, love unfeigned, kindness, and pure knowledge. Differences of opinion between a leader and a member are routinely treated as disobedience or lack of faith on the member's part and such differences are not resolved on the merits of the respective positions, but by making the issue a test of the member's loyalty. Saints who have concerns about church governance or doctrine are stigmatized as members in need of counsel or discipline. Ecclesiastical leaders are allowed to interfere with academic freedom, scholarly activity, and professional pursuits. And, perhaps worst of all, the church is fast evolving into a class-system of spiritual inequality based not only on church position but on gender discrimination that justifies the subordination of women in church governance, policy formation, and decision-making by discounting their contributions and devaluing their personal worth.

Most remarkable is that these wide-spread abuses are so invisible. Most Latter-day Saints refuse even to entertain the hypothetical possibility that such abuses exist. They cannot acknowledge or cope with them. They will either deny the evidence of them or rationalize that the church is true, God-ordained, God-directed, that its leaders are God-called and God-approved, and that God simply would not permit such abuses to infect the church. What problems, if any, that exist are attributed to the human imperfections of church members. Even members who have themselves experienced abuses or witnessed them first-hand in the lives of relatives or friends tend to deny or discount their significance, severity, and universality. Few are prepared to admit that such abuses are not the result of the personal foibles and failings of individuals but of the systemic failings of the church itself: from false teachings, false doctrines, false perceptions, and false practices.

All is not well in Zion. But what exactly is wrong? What is causing the plague of abuse afflicting the church? The cause is not, as some leaders suggest, the disobedience of members nor, as some members suggest, the personal foibles of leaders. The cause, I think, is suggested in the scripture: "Wo unto him that is at ease in Zion." Our dis/ease springs from those teachings about which our community feels most at ease, from our most treasured perceptions, our most assured assumptions, our most settled convictions. Our greatest heresy is the teaching we find least paradoxical, most straightforward, least tenuous, and most basic. Our greatest idol is in our holiest shrine.

I am not comfortable branding any teaching a heresy. I believe in speculative theology. I have co-authored a book full of such speculations. I do not believe a doctrine is heretical simply because it is unfamiliar, radical, or insufficiently supported by scripture or revelation. For me, a heresy is a teaching of the church that is significantly more likely to lead to evil than to good, that has a high probability of causing people to systematically perpetuate or exploit the weaknesses or powerlessness of others.

I believe that in Mormonism our chief idol is a false concept of God, a heresy which I call "patriolatry." It is the idolatry of God the Father. From this single heresy springs an unnumbered host of mischiefs and abuses, including—to name the most egregious—a false concept of salvation; false ideas about priesthood and authority; misunderstandings about church structure and membership; poisonous teachings about gender and sexuality; misconceptions about ordinances; and a false picture of Zion.

I do not doubt that in his fourteenth or fifteenth year Joseph Smith went into a grove of trees, prayed, and beheld a glorious theophany. I do not doubt that Joseph Smith saw Jesus Christ and other divine and angelic personages. What I do doubt, however, is the accuracy of the modern church's picture of God derived from this vision. My doubts arise because the church has ignored most of what Joseph Smith taught us about God. It has ignored the folk-magical context of the first vision, the strange angiology with which it is associated, and his later revelations about the nature, number, character, and roles of the Godhead. The church, oversimplifying God to the point of idolatry, now teaches that the main members of the Godhead are the Father and the Son, two separate and distinct beings with glorified bodies of flesh and bone, that the Father as the First Person in the Godhead is the superior, senior, and more-experienced deity, that the Son as the Second Person in the Godhead—though superior, older, and wiser than we—is in all matters subordinate and obedient to the Father, and that the Holy Ghost, not mentioned in the first vision but in later Mormon scriptures, is the least member of the trinity. Later extrapolations by leaders, especially the late apostle Bruce R. McConkie, have persuaded members to worship not the Son, but the Father—for he is supreme. Elder Boyd K. Packer has been persuasive in teaching that the plan of redemption is not the Son's plan, but the Father's. From the temple rituals, the church has adduced that the trinity is a chain of command. These teachings form the basis of patriolatry (or heavenly-fatherolatry), a God-concept that is concocted out of half-truths, misperceptions, and trivializations and that does no justice to the revelations or to the doctrinal richness of Mormonism. To erect this idol, it was necessary first to sweep away nearly all those complicated teachings, especially from the Book of Mormon, that identify Jesus as God of the Old Testament, as giver of the law of Moses, as both Father and Son, as the eternal God, the Father of heaven and earth, who condescends to appear to us as Son in order to make himself accessible to us and save us. Ignored is the teaching that Jesus is the everlasting Father of the resurrection and redemption and that we are called first to be his children through rebirth and then his friends through spiritual maturation. Christ is now depicted by the church as "elder brother," the subordinate rather than the equal of the Father. Patriarchal power is revered above redemptive power. Focus is on seniority rather than love, hierarchy rather than condescension. Authority is adored as the dominant divine characteristic, while sacrifice and humility are marginalized.

Utterly repressed from the Mormon God-concept are the teachings of Joseph Smith and Brigham Young that Michael the archangel is the father of our premortal spirits, that Michael came to earth as father Adam, that Michael entered into a covenant with Christ, the eternal God, in which each promised to serve as both the father and the son of the other in important ways. In the debates over the authenticity of this teaching, its power and Christocentricity have been completely lost.

The Adam-God doctrine is not about Adam. It is about Christ. Christ, the eternal God and father of heaven and earth, raised an archangel to divine status and then condescended to become the Son of that archangel. In so doing, Christ makes himself a little lower than the angels. He condescends to become the Son of his son. He agrees to make his son a Father, not only the progenitor of our spirits and mortal bodies, but the heavenly Father of Christ incarnate. In this covenant the power of patriarchy is broken, the children set free. Parent becomes the child of child, and child becomes parent of parent. The all-powerful yield up power to empower the weak beyond reckoning. Thereafter, Christ calls Michael "my Father who is in heaven," and Michael speaks to us of Christ in the gracious anthem: "This is my Beloved Son! Hear Him!" Thus, God not only makes himself equal to us, he makes himself less than we are, so we may be made equal to him. This is, in part, the meaning of the condescension of God.

Lost in the simplified God-concept of the modern church are the female divinities. Brigham Young taught that Eve is the mother of all living. She continues to be so denominated in the temple ceremony. "Mother of All Living" was the ancient epithet for the Great Goddess. Edward Tullidge, in his strange book *Women of Mormondom*, echoing Brigham Young, wrote not only that Eve is the Heavenly Mother, but that Mary Christ's Mother and Mary Magdalene, his spouse, also held divine status. Thus for her children's sake, Eve the Great Mother entered Eden as a daughter, yielding up her divinity to become the helpmeet of her son Adam. For her children's sake she sacrificed her glory and immortality to inhabit the dreary world. For their sakes she suffered death to wander in the earth as a light to them that dwell in darkness—the *Shekinah,* the *Hokma,* the paraclete, the Holy Spirit—rebirthing, nurturing, consoling, comforting, reproving, inspiring, defending, and blessing her children as they, poor banished children of Eve, cry weeping and wailing in this veil of tears.

Forgotten, too, are the wonderful stories of how Jesus

loved his female disciples, how he conversed with them, elected them, liberated and empowered them, and chose them against all the prohibitions of their law and culture to be witnesses of his incarnation, his messianic mission, his crucifixion, his resurrection, his forty-day ministry, and his ascension. Forgotten, too, is his requirement that wherever the gospel is preached the story should be told of how a woman, Mary of Magdala, was chosen to bestow on Jesus the last anointings essential for his final work of redemption and resurrection. For as one Mary provided him his earthly tabernacle, so another Mary provided him with the chrism of his calling. She was elected to be a high priestess to him. She is an archetype for all who are called to be priestesses of and to the Most High. For women too are clothed in the robes of the Melchizedek priesthood and may officiate in all its ordinances.

Forgotten is the promise that in the end time Christ the Bridegroom shall come. The Bride, the *Shekinah* or *Hokma,* shall be revealed in power with the moon under her feet and twelve stars in her crown. Father Michael, the ancient of days, shall sit. And Mary, the Mother of Christ, shall be honored in the Godhead. The Father-Mother-Son-Daughter shall be made one. In that time there shall be no more strangers, no more servants, no more parents, no more children, no more Muslims, nor Catholics, nor Protestants, nor Buddhists, nor Mormons either. All who have loved God shall be equals, friends, and lovers. We seem to have lost sight of the truth that our Mothers and Fathers in heaven yield up their glory, descend into mortality, suffer as sinners, and die so that we their children may be exalted. The greatest of all become the servants of all, while we whom they serve, not knowing what the Gods are like, are promised that, when the Gods are revealed, we shall see that we are like them for we shall see them as they are. For now, we are to think of ourselves as Adam and Eve. We are to walk in their footsteps, retracing their spiritual journey. Our purpose, like theirs, is not to accumulate power and honor, but to empower the powerless, to honor the dishonored.

All these teachings both leaders and members ignore or deny. Truly it may be said of us: Never have so many done so little with so much. In our desperate attempt to purchase the praise of the world, we have sold our tokens for money, our birthright for a mess of pottage. Instead of milk or meat, we content ourselves with the monotonous, thin, and inadequate gruel of patriolatry—the image of an all-male trinity ordered like cosmic corporate executives with the Father presiding as chairman of the board, the Son as his subordinate but still president of the corporation, and the Holy Ghost as their assisting chief executive officer. These trivializations of God are heretical not just because they are inaccurate (for all pictures of God fall short of the truth), but because their incompleteness and simplicity are contrived and imposed contrary to the will of God, because they lead inevitably to spiritual poverty, spiritual bondage, spiritual abuse, and spiritual death. Patriolatry is nothing but a composite of some of the most abusive characteristics of controlling, modern, middle-aged, white, Western males. It blows unimpeded through the church like a cold wind, chilling compassion, hope, and faith. It persists because it supports authoritarianism. Patriolatry promotes the authoritarianism that promulgates it. Like two drunks, they prop each other up.

Because God is pictured as patriarch, some church leaders believe they are justified in hammering us into subordination, in making us eternal children who must live forever under a patriarchal control we can neither outgrow nor outlive. Because patriolatry sees God as hierarch, it fortifies the notion of a leadership elite, appointed by God and grouped into councils and quorums ordered in ascending ranks of power, mimicking the seraphim and cherubim, and even the trinity itself, while claiming the ultimate power to govern and control, to judge and punish. Patriolatry makes our role clear: we are to obey our leaders, serve them, sustain them, sacrifice for them, and love them for the privilege. The worship of God, the commandment-giver, reinforces the church's claim to issue, multiply, and enforce commands as a way of preserving purity. The image of God as sacrificer of his Son serves as a model for the exercise of control over others, authorizing the church not only to demand sacrifices of its members, but to sacrifice its members in the interests of the church, its mission, its image. Because God is pictured as a sovereign without accountability, his leaders with little or no accountability may lay upon members the heavy burdens of guilt, confusion, depression, anger, doubt, rejection, alienation, fear, and spiritual abuse and not lift even the least of these with the littlest of their fingers.

Patriolatry then is the source of the modern church's false concept of priesthood and authority. In Mormonism, priesthood authority and power is derived from Jesus Christ, who sent angels to call and ordain the apostles of the restoration, giving them the power of the ancient apostles that whatsoever they should bind on earth should be bound in heaven and whatsoever they should loose on earth should be loosed in heaven. However, Christ has never given to any of his apostles the power to loose on earth what Christ has bound in heaven nor to bind on earth what Christ has loosed in heaven. Thus the apostles have no power to act contrary to the will of Jesus. They cannot change his words, his ordinances, his gospel. Priesthood is inseparably connected with the powers of heaven and cannot be used to oppose the spirit or will of God.

This view of priesthood as an authority that is limited by the will of Christ, divided among leaders and members, and balanced by the spiritual gifts is not the prevailing view of the current church leadership. That view was set forth by Elder Boyd K. Packer in his talk to the All-Church Coordinating Committee on May 18, 1993. There he set forth the source and pith of his theory of priesthood leadership. In 1955 Elder Packer, as a seminaries and institutes administrator, visited Elder Harold B. Lee in Salt Lake City. In this private meeting Elder Lee reportedly made an unelaborated comment that became the seed of Elder Packer's understanding of priesthood authority. Elder Lee said, in essence, that church administrators and local leaders should not advocate the causes of members to leaders, but the policies of leaders to members. Leaders are to lead, and followers are to follow. It is very simple. Elder Packer gave Elder Lee's comment the force of scripture and built his life of priesthood service around it. Elder Packer's advice to us is never to face our leaders in opposition, but to face the direction our leaders face without question.

Elder Packer does not consider in his talk that one may be loyal to both leaders and members by being loyal first to Christ Jesus and to the Holy Ghost. I am confident of this higher principal, in part, because I learned it from Harold B. Lee. For I too had a personal interview with Elder Lee in October 1966. I had a doctrinal question as I was leaving on my mission to Italy and found myself in Elder Lee's office. His advice to me was this: In order to test the truth of any inspiration, statement, or purported revelation—even of a church leader—it must be subjected to four tests: First, it must not be inconsistent with the scriptures; second, it must not be inconsistent with the teachings of the prophets living and dead; third, it must not be inconsistent with one's own spiritual promptings and experiences; and fourth, it must not be inconsistent with the principle of divine love. The fewer of these tests the claimed revelation or inspiration passed the less reliable it was. This means that members have the right and duty to put the claims of their leaders to the test. I accept this teaching not merely because Elder Lee told it to me, but because it itself is not inconsistent with scripture, with the teachings of the prophets living and dead, with my own spiritual feelings, and with the love of God.

There are those, like Elder Packer, who see it otherwise. They believe priesthood leadership is entitled to blind obedience without the application of these tests. Few are the members willing to oppose the view of Elder Packer and his protégés. Attempts to apply these four tests are dismissed or thwarted as dissent, opposition, or apostasy. Members who complain about coercive leadership are rebuked. Their letters to general authorities are returned to their stake presidents with instructions to call the members in. Those who continue to object are often intimidated, disciplined, and silenced. Once this happens, they are shunned as apostates by more conservative members, who numb themselves into believing blind obedience will keep them from being led astray. These members conveniently forget the track record of their leaders: Aaron built the golden calf. Moses was denied entrance into the promised land for taking glory to himself. Peter denied Christ three times. Joseph Smith promoted the ill-fated Kirtland Bank. Brigham Young taught that blacks were an inferior race. Wilford Woodruff held that the Second Coming would occur in the 1890s. J. Reuben Clark viewed Hitler positively even after the war began. Joseph Fielding Smith prophesied that men would never reach the moon. Bruce R. McConkie insisted that blacks would never get the priesthood. The First Presidency and Council of the Twelve supported the Vietnam War, mainly to preserve the church's patriotic image. Meanwhile, the church's image has received blow after blow from its leaders: Though President Ezra Taft Benson once urged members to be ultraconservative, Elder Malcolm Jeppson and others now seek to excommunicate those same members for their ultra-conservativism. Meanwhile, Elder Packer insists that feminists, homosexuals, and intellectuals should not be publicly comforted, but quarantined. Elder Dallin H. Oaks counsels the use of obsolete prayer language to encourage, not greater intimacy, but greater distance from and respect for God. Elder Russell Nelson suggests that whenever he or his apostolic brothers enter a room, members should stand. I agree. We *should* stand—and leave. Moses was told, "Take off the shoes of thy feet"—maybe we should just take off. Am I mocking? Yes, but not God. Besides, does not such elitism deserve to be mocked? Is there any doubt that our prophets do not always speak as prophets? Do we not all recall the photograph of the First Presidency and Elder Packer posing with Mark Hofmann and examining with approval the Hofmann forgeries they wrongly thought were authentic historical documents?

In spite of my harsh recital of their errors, I do not fault our leaders for these mistakes. We all err. We all fall short of our callings. No one is infallible. What I fault is the pretense that our leaders do not or cannot err on important questions. What I object to is the counsel that we always face the same way our leaders face. This admonition only promotes tunnel vision. To see the full compass of 360 degrees we must stand face to face. If we don't want our backs exposed, we must face each other. This does not have to be confrontational.

We can do so in a circle of love, a circle of friends, a circle of prayer. Even if we disagree, we can have good will and respect each others gifts. Why do we forget that prophesy is a gift, not an office? Why do we confuse the worship of God with obedience to leaders? to trust in the arm of flesh? Why do we let leaders rule as "lords over God's heritage" rather than examples to the flock? to feed upon rather than feed the sheep? to place barriers between us and God?

We do it because we live in a Descartesian silence where almost no one hears God anymore. We are desperate for prophets to link us with the divine because we hear little or nothing. This is unlike the view that obtained in the pagan or medieval worlds when people perceived God all around. We live in the declining decades of the Western world where the voice of God is blotted out by the sound of our inventions and our fears. We are much more desperate for God. So, we think we need prophets to maintain radio contact with deity. But this is not the true role of true prophets. True prophets are called to break down the illusion that we are isolated from God. Their job is to show us that we are all connected to God at all times, not to insinuate themselves between us and the Holy Spirit. Rather than teach us all to be prophets, they make us co-dependent on them, arresting our spiritual growth. We allow this because some of us, like some of them, prefer certainty over holiness, childishness over maturity, and the simplicity of idolatry over the complexity of truth and love. Yes, they encourage us to get personal revelation, but only the kind that confirms their authority, not the kind that tests it. The scripture warns us against this mistake. In Doctrine and Covenants 64:38-40 we read:

> For it shall come to pass that the inhabitants of
> Zion shall judge all things pertaining to Zion. And liars

and hypocrites shall be proved by them, and they who are not apostles and prophets shall be known. And even the bishop, who is a judge, and his counselors, if they are not faithful in their stewardships shall be condemned and others shall be planted in their stead.

Perhaps the worst effect of our false picture of God is that it has begotten a false concept of salvation. Emphasis on God the Father, rather than God the Son, has shifted our emphasis from the New Testament to the most legalistic parts of the Old. For this reason we see salvation in terms of obedience rather than faith, law rather than spirit, and works rather than grace. A story may illustrate my point: In my Salt Lake City ward, the following object lesson was given by a primary teacher to the small children in her class. The teacher handed to each child two new clothes pins, the kind that snap shut by the action of a spring. The teacher asked the children to hold the clothes pins open for a whole minute. Those who would keep this commandment, would receive a treat. Unfortunately, the clothes pins were brand new ones with stiff springs. The children tried hard, but not one of them could hold open a single clothes pin for the allotted minute. The teacher was crestfallen. No child had been able to keep the commandment. This would have been a perfect time to drive home a point about the unconditional love and grace of Jesus Christ. But instead the teacher sighed with mild exasperation and said, "Well, I'll go ahead and give you the treats anyway. But I want you to know that your Heavenly Father wouldn't do this." When I told this story to one church leader, he said: "She shouldn't have given them the treats. Now they'll think they don't have to do anything."

The message is loud and clear: Heavenly Father demands compliance. His love is conditioned on our obedience. This graceless soteriology is expressed by the oft-re-peated Sunday school slogan: Salvation is a gift, but eternal life is earned. This means that salvation from mortality through the resurrection is a gift given to us because we cannot resurrect ourselves. But redemption or eternal life, which is salvation from the punishment for sin, is something that must earned because, as many of us believe, it is in our power to receive, understand, and obey the commandments and to perfect ourselves through obedience. This concept of salvation is essentially a concept of self-atonement that is everywhere contradicted by Mormon scripture. It persists in the church because it is the soteriology of choice of the correlation department and based on the theory that salvation is a result of natural cause and effect rather than divine mystery: If we obey the commandments (the cause), then we will be saved (the effect). We fortify this view with anecdotes about how people can indeed become perfect at tithing, perfect at church attendance, perfect at temple attendance, perfect at obeying our leaders. We forget that we need to be cleansed not only from our sins, but from our inclination to sin, from our low IQs, our blindness, our lack of knowledge, bad judgment, our egocentricity, our poor memories, our weaknesses, our lack of energy, our tendency to simplify—in short, we must be saved from ungodliness.

Modern Mormonism's false concept of salvation refuses to see that the perfection of our spirits is just as mysterious and unachievable by human effort as the perfection of our bodies and that each is a product of the grace of God, not of human effort. This is made plain in the New Testament story of the palsied man who was brought before Jesus to be healed. Jesus said to him, "Son, thy sins be forgiven thee" (Matt. 2:5). The scribes, hearing it, said in their hearts: This man commits blasphemy. Jesus said to them: Which is easier? to forgive sins or heal the sick? To show you that the Son of Man has power to forgive sins, I will also heal this man's palsy. And he did. The scribes were enraged not because Jesus healed the man, but because he forgave him apart from the ritual and legal requirements of the law of Moses. What the scribes saw as blasphemy was the establishment by Christ of a mechanism of salvation based on the direct relationship between the individual and God, thereby rendering salvation free and without price (as declared by Isaiah) without the intercession of law, priest, or church. The Book of Mormon, consistent with the New Testament view, also teaches that salvation—both immortality and eternal life—is dependent only upon the healing power of Christ.

Salvation is available not through works but through grace. We receive this not by fear but by faith, not by obedience to law but by a change of heart, not by birth but by rebirth—of water and of the spirit of the living God. Yes, certain evil practices must be avoided. For Mormons certain ordinances of grace are to be received. But no one is empowered to prescribe the positive actions we must take to please God. We are to take in the breath of the spirit and walk in a newness of life, following the promptings of the Most High, without intercession. Obedience, works, and judgment are replaced by faith, hope, and charity. God is no longer our enemy but our lover. He loves us and comforts us in our sins, so he can save us from our sins. Without his unconditional prevenient love, we could not have faith, or hope, or charity. Repentance would be impossible. Our sins would remain. It is because God loved us while we were yet sinners that we have hope of a life without sin. It is on this very point that the church is unclear because we see God as the giver of the law rather than as the one in whom the law had its end, as sacrificer rather than as sacrifice, as prosecutor rather than as accused, as judge rather than as condemned.

The idolatry of the Heavenly Father is demeaning not only to the Son of God, but to the Holy Ghost, who—as the female member of the Godhead—provides us with hope, nurture, and comfort, as well as reproof, revelation, and charismatic or spiritual authority. Elder Packer addressed the issue of comfort on May 18, 1993. He read a portion of three letters from troubled Saints: the first, from a homosexual; the second, from a feminist; the third, from an intellectual—all seeking comfort from the church. Brother Packer then asked the following rhetorical question: "How can we give solace to those who are justified without giving license to those who are not?" In other words, he asks, how can the church comfort the clean without inadvertently comforting the unclean? In a drought of love, how can the church let the rain fall on the just, without letting it fall on the unjust? Elder Packer gave the simple answer: the church should not comfort such members—at least not publicly. In his view, the corporate church is exempt from Jesus' teachings: The church need not do good to its perceived enemies, or walk an extra mile with them, or give them a coat and a cloak, or turn the other cheek. The church, instead, must stick with the ninety and nine and resist the temptation to go after the one. In this counsel, the feminine aspects of God that long for and give hope to the lost, the prodigal, are denied; the Holy Spirit, quenched; the spiritual gifts, restricted; and personal spiritual experiences, marginalized—all in the interest of gratifying the church's insatiable and obsessive lust for purity.

This obsession has had poisonous effects on the modern Mormon view of gender and sexuality. Today, most leaders and members confuse sexual repression with chastity, and chastity with spirituality. Sexuality is viewed with envy and suspicion. Sexual pleasure is considered lewd and corrupting. Male sexual energy is acknowledged, but is shamed as weakness and repressed. Often it is channeled by men into the corporate church where it is transformed and emerges as self-control and control of others. In this way many Mormon men forfeit natural affection. Loyalty replaces love, interviews replace intimacy, fraternity replaces foreplay, rectitude replaces erections, and ordinations replace orgasms. Power entices with pornographic intensity. Men lust for authority, fantasizing not centerfolds of naked women, but organizational-charts and photo displays of leaders ranked in seniority order. Female sexual energy is ignored or denied. In a homocentric system where God the Father is pictured as having no significant contact with women, no need of women, no interest in women and as issuing commandments and revelations from a transcendence that appears utterly innocent of the existence, aspirations, or spirituality of women, the feminine becomes irrelevant. Women are of no interest, not even as the objects of desire. Joseph Smith had, obviously, a different view. Whatever may be said of him, he did not think women uninteresting. I believe he saw them as essential to the restoration and the exercise of the fullness of the priesthood. He taught that the fullness of the priesthood could be conferred only on men and women jointly, thus acknowledging that the priestly role of women is essential to the full manifestation of priesthood power. Patriolatry denies the priesthood role of women. It prefers an apostolic dispensation of males rather than the dispensation of the fullness of the male and female priesthoods.

Patriolatry is also destructive of community because it asserts that everything belongs to the leaders. Members have no rights, only privileges that are always conditioned on obedience. But this view flies in the face of scripture that tells us that salvation and exaltation are gifts of God, that priesthood is bestowed by revelation, and that these blessings vest in the Saints personally and are not privileges granted to us by mortals. They may not be taken from those of us who claim them by faith, by covenant. Church leaders do not keep the gate of heaven. The Lord is the keeper of the gate and employs no servant there (2 Ne. 9:41). Nor may these blessings be annulled or withdrawn arbitrarily to compel conformity. Any action to excommunicate a believing member for the purpose of coercing obedience to church leaders, church policy, or in the interest of church image is an abomination in the eyes of God, is utterly invalid, and will result in the de facto excommunication of the perpetrators who will suffer a withdrawal of the spirit and then amen to the priesthood of those leaders (D&C 121:37).

All is not well in Zion—not because some people are imperfect, but because there is a steady, relentless advancement of an heretical concept of God that fosters an ever-increasing tendency in church leaders to preach and interpret the gospel of Jesus Christ in legalistic and controlling terms thereby undermining the Saints' faith in Christ's unconditional love and power to save. I believe all Zion's ills, including spiritual abuse, spring directly or indirectly from modern Mormonism's oversimplified God-concept.

To combat idolatry it was once thought necessary to destroy the idols. Iconoclasm, however, does not usually result in the elimination of idolatry, but in the destruction of a lot of art work. Idolatry, after all, is not in the icon, but in the idolater. And since idolaters are people whom we are to love and respect, dealing with idolatry boils down to persuasion. This is tough work—principally because idolaters see themselves as guardians of true religion and view any attack upon it as persecution or apostasy. Discussions turn into arguments which turn into feuds which settle into permanent hostilities housed in schisms. What do we do?

First, we must not fear excommunication. I know our voices can be muted, even silenced by excommunication. But they can also be muted and silenced by our fear of excommunication. Either way, the silence works in favor of those abusing power. The choice is simple: Shall we silence ourselves or be silenced by others. I say let others do their own work. I will not live a life of self-imposed silence simply to avoid wrongful discipline. Second, we must admit that the modern church is a dysfunctional family: with some leaders in the role of abusive parents, some members in the role of brothers and sisters in denial, others are like siblings in exile, while others staunchly defend what they wish were true but is not. In this growing chaos, we must stand firm and tell the truth in love despite the pain. Third, we must continue to subject the teachings and practices of our leaders to the tests of scripture, prophets, personal spirituality, and charity. These tests cannot settle all differences. But there is no need for this. We need not settled questions but continuing revelation. We must see our religion in ever-fresh contexts, in ever-fresh readings, in ever-opening vistas of knowledge and experience. We should not seek to be at ease in Zion. We should glory in tribulations, live graciously with doubt, eschew rigidity, accept diversity, avoid complacency, comfort the afflicted, and afflict the comfortable. Only when Zion is uneasy with its sins and shortcomings can all be well.

Mormonism claims to be the true church restored as it was in the time of Christ. I believe in the restoration, but I do not believe it is complete. More must take place. This is suggested by the mythic structure of Mormon history: Joseph Smith, according to the Book of Mormon, was not a type of Peter or Paul but of Joseph who was sold into Egypt. Brigham

Young was a modern Moses, leading the exodus of the pioneer Saints. There is evidence that the first pioneers carried with them the body of Joseph Smith, even as the Israelites of old carried before them into the promised land the sarcophagus of Joseph of old. The Mormon promised land is strangely similar to the land of Israel—a desert with a dead salt sea connected to a fresh body of water by a river which the pioneers named the Jordan. Like ancient Israel, Mormons experienced a patriarchal period (complete with polygamy), then a period of settlement and expansion, then a period of temple building, then in the twentieth century a Talmudic-type period when teachings were developed and solidified. In broad strokes, Mormonism appears to be a microcosm of the mythic journey of the House of Israel. We seem to be approaching on that mythic continuum a time comparable to the time of Christ's birth. For now the church is a settled feature of America, even as Israel, two millennia ago, was a fixture of the Roman Empire. In the modern church we have zealots, essenes, sadducees, pharisees, and far flung members like Jews in the diaspora. We also have ever-increasing numbers of members who are looking for inner life, for renewal, for the coming of the Christ—even as the pre-Christian Jews looked for deliverance, for peace, for the coming of the Messiah. The grand themes of Israel's story seem to have been recapitulated in Mormon history. Is this the prelude to some apocalypse? If so, what could it be? In the words of William B. Yeats: "What rough beast, its hour come round at last,/ Slouches toward Bethlehem to be born?" ("Second Coming," 1920-21)

The Heavenly Father was revealed 4,000 years ago, and the Redeeming Son 2,000 years ago. Could it be time now for the revelation of the Bride, the Comforting Woman of Holiness, the Lady, the Queen of queens and of her connection to the earth, the environment, the heavens, the angels, and the Father and the Son whom we have heretofore worshipped? Could we be standing on the eve of a second restoration, when—as the Book of Mormon prophesies—the Lord shall "set his hand *again* the second time to recover his people" (2 Ne. 25:17; 29:1)? Must the same Goddess who in the beginning condescended first be in the end unveiled last? Must She, the last God to be worshipped, be the first to come again as part of the final parousia?

I cannot say. I say only that all is not well—nor is it likely ever again to be well—in Zion. For unless there is a spiritual revival of mythic dimensions, the restoration, I fear, is doomed to resolve itself into yet another sect full of ethical pretensions and xenophobic aspirations—and nothing more. But if we Saints can be shaken from our idolatries, but if we can be roused from our fawning fascination with ourselves, but if we can abandon our obsession with power and patrio-latry—"but if our lives are spared again, to see the Saints their rest obtain, O how we'll make this chorus swell: All is well, all is well."

Chapter Ten.

ON LOVE

"On Love" was delivered on 5 December 1993 at a gathering sponsored by the Olive Branch, an ad hoc committee organized to publish in The Salt Lake Tribune *a 28 November 1993 notice expressing support for those excommunicated, disfellowshipped, and otherwise disciplined by the church for their religious opinions.*

"For God has not given us the spirit of fear, but of power, and of love, and of a sound mind" (2 Tim. 1:7). In spite of this reassuring scripture, there is fear among us—even though God is not the giver of it. At the same time, there seems to be so little love. Have you ever noticed this? How little love there is among the Latter-day Saints? There is obedience, of course, and service. There is sacrifice and restraint. We are responsible, clean, conscientious, a little clannish, hard-working and healthy, righteous and reliable, often sentimental and sometimes naive. Many non-Mormons say that we make good neighbors, but poor friends. Chiefly, we are known for being nice. Not for being loving.

Last week I was talking religion with three disaffected Mormons in their early twenties. They asked me what the core of my beliefs was at this point in my life. "Grace," I said.

"I've banked everything on the grace of God—on God's unconditional love."

One of the two young men scowled at me. "How I hate unconditional love," he said. This was an interesting and unexpected response. I asked him why.

"Because that's what my parents always say—that they love me unconditionally, that no matter what I say, or think, or do I will always be part of their eternal family."

"This is bad?" I asked, pressing him.

"Yes," he said with visible energy. "They don't really know me, what I think, how I feel. They don't want to hear about the experiences I've had because they are not the experiences I should have had as a Mormon. They don't want to hear about my questions, my doubts, my views. They just want me to smile, show up at family gatherings, and fill the place they've made for me in their eternal family. They don't love me as a person. They love me only as a role."

"Yes," I said. "It's like the way some people love the homeless. It's a lot easier to love them as a group when you don't actually have to know and deal with any of them personally." We talked about how much easier it is to love in a general way the ideal of the family, the church, the country than it is to love any of the specific individuals that make up those groups. This is how some Mormons love the church without loving any of its members. I was reminded then of a remark made by Elder Dallin Oaks. When he was told that many people of the 1960s' generation were losing their faith, he responded: "Well, it won't hurt the Church." He was thinking, of course, of the collective—not the individual struggling Saints. He had lost sight of the body of Christ, where damage done to one member is damage done to all. He was, perhaps, thinking of the church as a beehive or an anthill or even a machine in which the loss of a few cogs is insignificant since there are so many of them—each one fungible, replaceable, dispensable. Perhaps, momentarily, Elder Oaks forgot Jesus' statement: "As you have done it unto the least of these, you have done it unto me."

This isn't really love, of course. It is sentimentality. Sentimentality is affectionate and emotional, but it keeps itself at a distance. It makes no permanent attachments. It is without commitment, without depth, without meaning. For this reason, sentimentality is usually found in the service of authoritarianism. Tyrants are almost always sentimental. They think in terms of the welfare of the collective, not of individuals. They love Catholicism not Catholics. They are loyal to Germany not Germans. They are devoted to Israel not Jews, Palestine not Palestinians. They love the "one and only true"—whatever they may imagine it to be—but they do not love seekers after truth.

Sentimentality is the partner of compulsion because it lacks the most critical component of true love. It lacks passionate and specific desire for another, the desire we feel as inexpressible attachment or unfulfillable longing—the untamed devotions and desires that draw us beyond our cherished settled categories into the unpredictable, unknown, mysterious, and dangerous realms of another's heart. As a people, we Latter-day Saints are schooled all our lives to distrust and avoid such desire, such attachment, such passion. We do not give our hearts easily. Nor do we accept the hearts of others. We prefer the safety, the certainty, the sanity of sentimentality. For sentimentality allows us to enjoy lukewarm feelings that can never boil over, relationships without risk, pleasantries without pleasure, and poignancies without pain. Sentimentality allows us to preserve ourselves against the change that must inevitably follow the true love of another.

The way we Mormons justify our resistance to change is by invoking the icon of purity. We say we want to keep ourselves, our families, our institutions, our doctrines pure. What we mean is that we want to avoid changing our minds. We want to preserve ourselves and our views in a condition that is static, unadulterated, and unmixed—a state that is utterly innocent of the experiences, hopes, and fears of others. Our obsession with purity is the foundation of our judgmental view of the world. In the name of purity we justify our exercise of control—self-control and control of others. In the name of purity, we seek to alter our environment—physical, spiritual, psychological—so we do not have to be altered ourselves. In the name of purity, we avoid repentance. For the pure need no repentance and no forgiveness. From the high tower of our purity, we look down in detached serenity at those who are not so wholesome, not so correlated as we are. We can pity them, invite them to be like us, advise them, admonish them, threaten them, exclude them, and even damn them. But we are never touched by them because we are not joined to them—not deeply, not permanently. In the words of Elder Neal Maxwell, "we need them not" or "we heed them not." It does not matter which phrase he uttered. The point is the same. We are not part of them. They are not part of us. Our purity protects us. It is the ultimate prophylactic.

True love, whose essence is passionate devotion and unquenchable desire, is the enemy to all control. It breaks upon us without warning. Like a deluge, it overflows the banks of our righteousness. It sweeps away respectability, turns dignity into mud, lays waste the levees of our vaunted invulnerability. It pours into us, filling us with the longing to be longed for, the desire to be desired, the urge to know another and to be known by another, to embrace and be embraced, to join and be joined, to enter and yet to encircle, to be made hungry by what most satisfies. Call it what you will—eros, philia, agape—it does not really matter. At heart, these loves are all one. And when felt in the pith of the center of the soul of our being, love breaks down the tower of judgment, undermines the foundations of control, and washes away the walls of detachment. It lays open our shame and exposes us to pain, not only our own, but the pain and shame felt by those we love, and those they love, and those they love. It leaves us changed, repentant, and forgiving. It leaves us connected and unprotected. It leaves us contaminated with holiness.

True love is open, equal, reciprocal, specific, intimate, intense, knowing, forgiving, repenting, hopeful, sacrificial, passionate, and desiring. It sees beauty not just in form but in content. It is guileless and vulnerable. It abandons control and embraces mystery. It leaps away from ego and into the soul of the unknown, into the heart of the divine.

Is it any wonder that we Mormons fear it so? And the fear of love casts out love, just as much as the love of love casts out fear. In our weakness and our poverty, we do not seek love. We reject it. We reject the emptiness that longs to be filled. We reject the fullness that longs to be emptied. Instead, we seek substitutes that have the form of love, but deny its power and mystical beauty.

The call of God to us—through the prophets, through Christ, through the intercession of the Holy Spirit—is that we love one another as God loves us: passionately, specifically, unconditionally, as equals, without injury, compulsion, dominion, or control. The call of God to us is that we repent of our fear, that we truly be with one another, even as God is with us through the Spirit. To withhold love is the greatest sadness. To give it in the full measure we are able and to receive it in the full measure we are able is the greatest joy. Thus, we go from grace to grace until we are filled with love and a perfect brightness of hope. And, as Joseph Smith said, those who are filled with such love can never fall.

Tonight, many have gathered here in support of a few. But that is not the whole of it. We are all one body. Damage done to one is damage done to all. Even as you have felt our pain, we have felt yours. But I hope that you can also feel our love. I, for one, feel your love. This is the purpose of the gospel that we love one another as God has always loved us, that we may be made whole, and complete, and one. May we pass beyond the darkness of fear into the marvelous light of God's love. May God bless us all in the name of Christ our Father and the Spirit our Mother.

EPILOGUE

*The following prayer was given as the closing prayer at the B.
H. Roberts Society meeting held at the University of Utah on Friday,
17 September 1993.*

Gracious Father and Blessed Mother: What a strange picture
we must present before your eyes. We know our attitudes are
generally unacceptable, our voices are alternate, and our
beliefs are unorthodox. We are, on the whole, a diverse and
motley crew. What unites us is hard to say—except, perhaps,
our pain, our love for each other, and our desires and
longings for truth, love, justice, and mercy.

As for the Restoration, it seems to be in such a hopeless
state. And those who should see this most seem to notice it
least. It is as if you have forsaken us.

O Lord and Lady, draw near to our community again.
Let some of the eternal fire of your everlasting burnings peel
the whitewash off the church. Pull back the draperies. Let in
the light. Shake out the dust covers. Rid us of the partitions
and the bureaucratic little cubicles. Tear down the false
ceilings and make the grand old scrollwork visible again.
Retrieve the forgotten arts and return the beautiful books.
Send to lead us kind, wise men of patience and faith and

women full of knowledge and no nonsense. Restore our appetites and passions, our faith and hope. Fill us with benign contempt for mediocrity. Give us courage in the face of coercion. Forgive those who think we are their enemies. Forgive us our trespasses. Fill us with divine love. And when trials come—and we know they must—deliver us from evil.

For these things we pray with sincerity of heart through the intercession of the Holy Spirit and in the name of Jesus Christ. Amen.

About the Author

Paul James Toscano, an attorney associated with the Salt Lake City law firm of Woodbury & Kesler, has practiced law since 1978 and currently serves as Chapter 12 and Chapter 13 Standing Bankruptcy Trustee for the District of Utah. He received his B.A. and M.A. degrees in English from Brigham Young University and his J.D. from the J. Reuben Clark Law School. He is author/co-author of numerous articles and four books: *Gospel Letters to a Mormon Missionary, Invisible Religion in the Public Schools: Secularism, Neutrality, and the Supreme Court, Music and the Broken Word* (with Calvin Grondahl), and *Strangers in Paradox: Explorations in Mormon Theology* (with Margaret Merrill Toscano). He is the founder and co-president with Margaret of the Mormon Alliance, a non-profit corporation organized in 1992 to counter defamation of and spiritual abuse in the LDS church. A 1963 convert from Catholicism, he was excommunicated on 19 September 1993 as one of the September Six.